**A NUCLEAR REACTOR DEEP IN
THE NEGEV DESERT . . .**
where Israel's most secret and heavily guarded
project was threatened with imminent disaster

**THE INTELLIGENCE NERVE-CENTER
IN TEL AVIV . . .**
where a desperate gamble was hotly debated, then
cold-bloodedly worked out

A PARIS BEDROOM . . .
where an Italian scientist plunged into an orgy
of sexual pleasure whose price he only later would
discover

AN ANTWERP WAREHOUSE . . .
where two teams of rival agents fought a
nightmare gun battle

**A SEALED CONTAINER IN A
SHIP'S HOLD . . .**
where four dedicated men crouched, awaiting the
precise moment to break out of their steel cocoon

A NARROW GREEK ISLAND COVE . . .
where a ship could find sanctuary—if jagged
rocks didn't rip her hull wide open

THE OPEN MEDITERRANEAN . . .
where the only route to Israel was through a
searching armada of hostile naval vessels and planes

OPERATION URANIUM SHIP

*the riveting true story of a mission impossible
that can now be revealed!*

Big Bestsellers from SIGNET

OPERATION URANIUM SHIP

by Dennis Eisenberg,
Eli Landau,
and
Menahem Portugali

A SIGNET BOOK

NEW AMERICAN LIBRARY

TIMES MIRROR

NAL BOOKS ARE ALSO AVAILABLE AT DISCOUNTS IN BULK QUANTITY
FOR INDUSTRIAL OR SALES-PROMOTIONAL USE. FOR DETAILS, WRITE TO
PREMIUM MARKETING DIVISION, NEW AMERICAN LIBRARY, INC.,
1301 AVENUE OF THE AMERICAS, NEW YORK, NEW YORK 10019.

SIGNET TRADEMARK REG. U.S. PAT. OFF. AND FOREIGN COUNTRIES
REGISTERED TRADEMARK—MARCA REGISTRADA
HECHO EN CHICAGO, U.S.A.

SIGNET, SIGNET CLASSICS, MENTOR, PLUME AND MERIDIAN BOOKS
are published by The New American Library, Inc.,
1301 Avenue of the Americas, New York, New York 10019

First Signet Printing, February, 1978

1 2 3 4 5 6 7 8 9

PRINTED IN THE UNITED STATES OF AMERICA

*This book is dedicated
to some brave men and women*

Foreword

This book is in essence the true story of how a cargo of uranium vanished on the high seas in 1968. It was an event which remained a secret until the summer of 1977 when the bare details were revealed at an antinuclear conference in Austria.

As a result of this public disclosure, the authors no longer felt prohibited from describing what happened to the uranium. In order to protect the lives and reputations, as well as the security, of many of the people involved, real names are not always used. The dialogue cannot be totally accurate after all this time, but it is as authentic as possible, given the literary licence needed to maintain the narrative.

In Salzburg, Austria, Mr. Paul Leventhal, a former American Senate committee expert on the spread of nuclear weapons, revealed that 200 tons of uranium had vanished in 1968.

Mr. Leventhal, speaking at an antinuclear conference on April 29, 1977, said the uranium had disappeared at sea somewhere between Antwerp and Genoa.

"It is assumed that it was unloaded in Israel."

> Although investigations by at least four nations have never officially resolved the mystery of the disappearance, some American and European intelligence agencies are convinced that the uranium found its way to Israel, which since 1963 has possessed a reactor capable of creating the raw material of atomic bombs—*The Times,* London, April 30, 1977

> E.E.C. [Common Market] authorities have been deeply embarrassed by the revelation of the missing uranium. It was under the supervision of Euratom inspectors at the time of its disappearance.—*The Daily Telegraph,* May 5, 1977

Israel has the capability of making H-bombs. There is speculation that the story of the uranium disappearance has been deliberately leaked to back up President Carter's campaign to stop the spread of nuclear weapons.—*Daily Mirror*, April 30, 1977

An Israeli agent confessed to police in Norway that he helped in an operation to divert 200 tons of uranium to Israel about nine years ago, Mr. Haakon Wiker, a former Norwegian chief prosecutor said.—Reuters News Agency, May 8, 1977

"We don't know whether there ever was such a shipment of uranium, and if there was, it had absolutely nothing to do with Israel."—An official of the National Atomic Energy Commission of Israel

"We deny all aspects of the story which relate to Israel," said a spokesman for the Commission when asked about the shipment of uranium

The denial was repeated by the acting Prime Minister, Mr. Shimon Peres

Chapter One

The high-pitched scream of the siren sliced the desert air with the fury of a howling genie suddenly released from a stone jar after centuries of imprisonment. The alert was totally unexpected. The sun burned down with terrible summer intensity. It seemed to regard the nuclear reactor as a particular target for daring to compete with its own vast powerhouse of heavenly energy. So searing were the light and heat bouncing off the silver dome that the staff at Dimona had to avert their eyes for fear of going blind—or mad.

The desert, so still and empty only seconds before, now burst into agitated life. From all directions men came running. Men rubbing the siesta from their eyes. Men buttoning their shirts. Men tightening their belts. Men strapping on helmets. One after the other, they leaped into trenches to take up well-rehearsed positions. This was the "on-duty" squad of hand-picked specialists who manned the Hawk missile batteries. Their job was to resist aerial attack against Israel's most precious and secret scientific asset: the nuclear reactor at Dimona in the Negev Desert.

The white-coated scientists in their nearby laboratories continued working calmly as though nothing had happened. The neighboring houses and low buildings where many of the technicians worked were as still as lizards sleeping in the shimmering heat.

From their trenches, however, the soldiers gazed expectantly into the blue sky. They were alert—ready to spring into action. Instinct warned them that this was no routine exercise designed to test their readiness. It was the real thing. Every single man in the squad knew it.

The siren was silent now. The only sound that could be heard was the thin, hissing movement of the revolving radar antennae probing impersonally into space.

In the control room, Lieutenant Daniel Gordon gripped the radar screen in front of him so tightly that his knuckles stood out white against the deep tan of his hands and forearms. His eyes were riveted to the warning, signaling its message loud and clear. He hardly dared blink. As though hypnotized, he watched the slow but steady progress of the bright yellow dot on the dial. The menacing speck had appeared a mere thirty seconds before, heading directly for the officially designated MPZ (Missile Protected Zone), or "Red Zone." This was an area that was strictly out of bounds to all civilian and military aircraft.

Surely it was a mistake. Maybe the radar was faulty. *Every* pilot knew it was tantamount to suicide to fly in this area. The yellow signal moved steadily on a dead straight path. It showed not the slightest variation.

The moment the radar had registered the alien object penetrating its air space, the operator had automatically pressed the alarm button, just as he had been trained to do. Now, recovering from his initial surprise, the lieutenant felt a sudden elation. What wonderful luck! For once, he had the good fortune to be on duty when it really mattered. It would be a moment to cherish for the rest of his life!

With a violence that almost ripped the door from its hinges, Colonel Gideon Eshet burst into the control room. His shirt was still unbuttoned, his hair uncombed. Breathing hard, he half ran, half leaped toward the radar screen, almost knocking Daniel Gordon from his seat. It took the trained eye of the colonel only a fraction of a second to grasp the message on the dial before him.

His hand shot out toward the red telephone standing on its own isolated platform to the right of the control panel. He jerked the receiver from its cradle so fiercely that the lieutenant half feared the connecting cord would be snapped right off.

It was the second day following the outbreak of the 1967 Six-Day War between Israel and the surrounding Arab states. Like everyone else at Dimona, Colonel Eshet listened to every hourly radio broadcast in order to follow the course of the battles then raging in the Sinai against the Egyptians, as well as to the north, in the Golan Heights.

Here at Dimona, tucked away in its secret, isolated corner of the desert, far from the eyes of curious tourists and foreign diplomats, the front line had seemed a long way off. Now the tiny, menacing blob on the screen meant only one thing. Dimona *was* the front line. That yellow speck was the approaching enemy. The intruder was fast-flying—a modern jet. It was coming for them like a winged arrow—dead on target to strike at the reactor. The colonel and his battery of missiles faced their supreme test. Would they be able to protect Israel's atomic city?

General Meir Amit, the head of the Mossad, Israel's intelligence service, was halfway through a sentence when the red telephone at his side rang shrilly. He reached for the receiver mechanically and, with a forced smile, to try and hide the sudden stab of apprehension that set every nerve in his body on edge, he turned to the colonel from the military branch of intelligence, sitting next to him, and said, "Here's the bad news we can do without right now!"

The eight men seated around the polished teak table in the long, narrow room held their breath. They all knew that the red telephone served only one purpose: to announce an emergency at Dimona. Eight pairs of eyes watched Meir Amit lift the receiver; they studied every line of his face, praying that it was all a mistake and that a look of relief would wash over the taut, pale features of the Mossad director.

They saw the lips of the intelligence chief move. But

even before they heard his words they could tell that potential disaster faced them. A pink flush appeared on his cheeks. They could see his jaw tighten with sudden tension.

Never a man of many words, he was now even less communicative than usual. He issued a few short commands, then slowly, almost as though in a trance, he replaced the receiver in its cradle. For a second or two, he looked around the room. The silence was total. Letting out a deep breath, more a grunt of expelled air than a sigh, he leaped to his feet and rushed to the door of the room.

"Get me the air force commander on the hot line! Now! Immediately!"

Dafna, his secretary, reacted calmly but swiftly. Meir Amit did not even look in her direction to see whether she was following his instructions. Her steadiness during crisis after crisis over the years had been proved time and again.

Regaining his seat, Meir Amit looked at the men around him. In a dry, harsh voice, he said: "An unidentified object, apparently a plane, is approaching the nuclear reactor from the northeast."

The eight individuals gathered before him had lived with danger for most of their lives. From time to time, all of them had been forced to make instant decisions which meant survival or death, not only for themselves but for the hundreds and thousands who served under them.

Even so, the news stunned them. They could hardly believe the extraordinary chain of events to which they had just been witness. Thirty minutes before the red phone had rung, a disturbing message had been brought to this very room: "The French government has decided that the embargo on shipments of military equipment to Israel will include uranium as well." France, who had helped them to build the atomic center, had suddenly turned off the tap. Without uranium, the silver-domed reactor would be totally paralyzed. They had half-expected this sellout. That was why they were here.

The meeting had been called to try and find a solution to an impossible problem: how to keep the nuclear reactor fed with uranium. It explained the presence of two of the country's leading scientists. The Prime Minister had issued an order: "Dimona *must* continue to function, no matter

6

what the circumstances—or the costs!" He could not have been more specific.

With a bitter smile on his lips, one of the men had turned to the Bible to curse President Charles de Gaulle for suddenly betraying Israel. "That son of a bitch could not have hit us harder if he had ordered one of his own planes to fly here and wipe Dimona from the face of the earth." Hardly had these words left his mouth than his listeners were faced with the astonishing reality that an aircraft *was* heading straight for the reactor.

Now the green phone beside Meir Amit began to ring. The voice of Colonel Shaike Bareket, intelligence commander of the air force, came over so clearly that those sitting nearest the chief could hear his every word. Not that he had much chance to express himself, for Meir Amit dominated the conversation.

"Dammit! What's happened to you? Has your radar cover gone to sleep?"

As he listened to the reply, the Mossad chief blinked in disbelief and his voice became hoarse and agitated.

"How can that be?" he exclaimed. "How in God's name can you explain that an aircraft is approaching the reactor from the northeast without one of your pilots intercepting it and shooting it down!"

He scarcely paused for the answer.

"I thought you had command of the skies! That's what you keep boasting about on the radio!"

Now it was the turn of the air force man to become agitated. He could be heard speaking in short, quick sentences. The way his voice rose in pitch revealed the strain he was under.

The face of General Meir Amit reflected stunned shock. It was though he had been slapped hard. His lips tightened, and unconsciously he raised his hand to his forehead in a gesture of despair. He did not even wait for the conversation to end before putting the receiver down.

His onlookers stared at him uncomprehendingly. What was going on? There was a feeling of impending doom in the smoke-filled room.

The chief of the Mossad fixed his gaze on an invisible spot on the opposite wall. As though speaking to himself, he whispered half audibly: "We are in trouble. Trouble that only the devil himself could have invented."

Ironically it *was* a French-built Super-Mystère whose path was now flickering on Lieutenant Daniel Gordon's screen. It was nearing the Dead Sea on its flight southwestward and it was slowly losing altitude.

From the earphones, which were dangling slightly in front of the young pilot's head, a metallic voice crackled monotonously:

"Eagle to Sparrow . . . Eagle to Sparrow . . . Eagle to Sparrow . . . Do you hear me? Over . . ."

"Eagle to Sparrow . . . Break to the right! Sparrow, this is Eagle . . . Over . . ."

Unheedingly the Super-Mystère continued to lose height.

Captain Yoram, the pilot, did not hear the voice beseeching him to answer. He heard nothing. His chest heaved irregularly beneath his parachute harness. His hands hung limply at his sides.

A large hole gaped at the base of his neck. The blood did not flow evenly from the open wound. It spurted in little jets, draining the life-force from the leader of the two-plane unit which had formed part of a larger squadron.

Yoram had been born in Israel, a "Sabra," the son of a Polish Jew who had emigrated with his family to the Promised Land. Slenderly built, shy and reserved, Yoram was married but had no children as yet. He had attended a religious school before going to high school. He had not been an outstanding pupil, except in Bible classes, where he always was first, although he was not particularly religious. And ever since his friends could remember, he had been crazy about planes. His eyes would light up as he explained to his classmates for the hundredth time how an aircraft worked and managed to stay airborne. He could rattle off details and specifications of almost every kind of aircraft in the world, in the same way that other boys his age knew everything about their favorite football team.

Yoram had joined the air cadets as soon as he was old enough, so no one was particularly surprised, when it was time for him to do his national service, that he volunteered for the air force. The day he was accepted as a pupil pilot, after passing rigorous physical and psychological tests, was the most joyous moment in his life.

Now Yoram was dying.

The anti-aircraft shell fired more in hope than expectation by a Jordanian army unit at the armada of French-built planes thundering by overhead could not have been better directed if it had been unleashed during target practice from close range. It had pierced the plane's belly, sliced through the pilot's back, and then emerged at the base of his neck.

Second-Lieutenant Gideon Barak had spotted the hit registered against his commander's plane. He had noticed the telltale tremble of the Super-Mystère, but since it continued to fly on a straight course, he assumed that the damage had been slight. Certainly his leader had given no sign that he had been injured.

Dead on schedule, the fleet of planes had struck earlier at H3, the major Iraqi air base nearest to Israel across the Jordan desert. In the opening hours of the war, Iraq's number one pilot, a colonel, had penetrated the Jewish state's defenses and, single-handed, had bombed several cities, including Nathania, killing one civilian—a woman. Belatedly, fighters rose to challenge him. The colonel paid with his life when the anti-aircraft fire downed him near Afula.

The Israeli air force had wreaked vengeance against H3, hitting dozens of Russian-built MIGs on the ground. The raid was so devastating that the Baghdad government got the message loud and clear and decided not to take any further action in the Six-Day War. Heading westward now that the mission was completed, the Mystère and Mirage fleet followed their squadron leader home.

Suddenly Gideon Barak heard an inhuman gurgle in his earphones. Yoram's plane started losing altitude. "It didn't change course, it didn't dive. It didn't go into a spin," he explained afterward. "It just lost height, slowly, as if the pilot was still in control."

Second-Lieutenant Barak tried the communication system. Again and again he called out the commander's code name. But in vain. He approached closer and closer until his plane's wings were almost touching those of his good friend Yoram's. Now he could see the pilot's helmet slumped forward, his face angled down, away from his instrument panel.

Gideon Barak felt icy fingers of fear in his throat and stomach. This was the sixth bombing mission he had been involved in since the war started before dawn on the 5th of June. As in all previous engagements, he was second in command to Captain Yoram. Together, they had bombed Egypt and Syria, hitting countless aircraft and other ground targets. They had fought aerial battles and dodged missiles aimed in their direction. At times they were mere seconds from death. With his own ears he had heard the cries of wounded pilots ejecting from hit planes—both Israeli and Arab. But like everyone else in a war he was convinced that it would never happen to him. To others maybe, but not him. In any event, he had total confidence in Yoram and his lightning reactions to every emergency they had encountered.

Now a frantic Gideon Barak called his base. "He has lost consciousness. He has lost control!" he yelled into his radio mouthpiece. "Do something, dammit!" The second-lieutenant's voice was high-pitched with anxiety.

In the control tower, many miles away, they plotted Barak's precise location, aware that he seemed disoriented and almost panic-stricken. He was now yelling almost non-stop into the mouthpiece. "Do something! Do something!" he repeated over and over again. "He's losing altitude . . ."

The flight commander's voice cut in sharply in mid-sentence. Calmly, as though talking to a child, he said gently: "Take it easy. Listen to me, Sparrow Two. You must try and rouse him. Try and get closer. Try to attract his attention any way you can. You are entering a Missile Protected Zone. I repeat. You are entering an MPZ area. . . . Sparrow Two. Do you read me?"

Second-Lieutenant Barak tried to get even closer to the stricken plane. As he edged ahead slightly, he could see the wounded man's face was streaked with blood. There was blood everywhere, on his chest, on his hands. Suddenly Yoram's plane shuddered slightly. The two aircraft were inches away from collision.

The ground controller's voice came through now hard and urgent, nearly bursting Barak's eardrums. "Sparrow

Two . . . Break to the right immediately. You are entering a Red Zone. I repeat. You are in a Red Zone. Break to the right. NOW!!"

The young pilot forgot himself for a few seconds and tried to argue.

The voice of his wing commander, Sumack, burst in. Stern with authority, he thundered: "Second-Lieutenant Barak. Break to the right. That's an order. Break immediately to the right. Return immediately to base. We will take care of Number One."

In the Hawk missile battery control room at Dimona, Colonel Gideon Eshet sat watching the dot of yellow light approaching on the screen. He had no doubt about it whatsoever. A supersonic plane was heading straight for the reactor.

He cursed out loud, his voice angry: "What are they waiting for, dammit!" He had total confidence in the American-built Hawk weapons at his disposal. He knew the capabilities of every single man under his command. There was no aircraft in the world that could slip past the wall of lethal fire they could send hurtling into the blue sky overhead at the press of a button.

But instead of being allowed to take action, he had to sit here helplessly and stare at a radar screen. He had requested permission to "act according to standard procedure," which they had all practiced again and again, so often that they could virtually carry it out in their sleep. The missiles were already aimed—following the radar target. Now when it mattered, when the occasion had arisen to launch his missiles, he was confronted with procrastination and repeated orders to hold his fire.

Suddenly, as though the screen had stretched out fingers to mock him, the yellow spot of light split in two before his very eyes. Now there were two specks pulling apart quickly. What was happening? Had the Russians given a new kind of secret weapon to their Arab partners to use in a Middle East war? Was it one of those multiple warheads he had heard about?

It was nothing of the kind, although Colonel Gideon Eshet could not know that. The second dot on the screen was Barak responding to the discipline that had been drummed into him during intensive training. He had

11

finally "broken to the right" as ordered. He had abandoned Yoram his friend and was heading back to base, his heart heavy with grief.

Again the colonel lifted the red receiver. General Meir Amit quelled the verbal outburst from Eshet about the "dithering." "Yes, I know." He cut the missile commander short. Briefly the Mossad chief explained the dilemma he faced. The jet approaching Dimona carried in its cockpit one of Israel's crack pilots, wounded and unconscious. They were trying to save him, trying to do everything possible to avoid the ultimate tragedy: shooting down the Super-Mystère and killing Yoram for sure.

"At the moment the only thing for you is to maintain a total alert," said Amit. "If we have to do it finally, then so be it. But it's better that your boys don't know who they are firing at. Keep it to yourself."

A man of medium height, General Meir Amit had a long bulldog face, a wide forehead, and steel-gray eyes. Like Yoram, he had been born in Israel. For a fraction of a second he thought of having one day to face the parents and wife of that pilot out there now, mortally wounded, in his jet crossing the Dead Sea. Angrily he dismissed the way he was already trying to find the inadequate words of apology and explanation he would need to utter to Yoram's family. It was the first time in his long military career and his service as head of intelligence that he felt the awful responsibility almost too much to bear.

Yet only a short while before he had been as overjoyed as the other senior officers at the war news reaching them. Parachute units had already broken through to the outskirts of East Jerusalem. Armored forces, after clashing headlong with King Hussein's tanks, were scattering the Arab armies to the winds. Victory against the Egyptians and Syrians was assured too, following the virtually total destruction of their air forces.

Now the sweet taste of success was turning sour in his mouth. All his thoughts were centered on the lonely plane approaching quickly, out of control, heading straight for the center of a "place" that did not even officially exist, that was not marked on any map. Its very name, from the Hebrew word *Dimion* ("fantasy"), underlined its mysterious function.

Dimona was Israel's atomic city. For a long time, foreign newspapers had spoken about Dimona, about its reactor, and inevitably there were reports—always denied—that its scientists were capable of building their own atomic weapons.

General Meir's responsibility was to protect the nuclear reactor. He also had a moral responsibility to try and save the life of the lonely, wounded pilot unconsciously threatening Dimona in his French plane, over which he no longer had any control. The thought had crossed Amit's mind: "How would I feel if he was my own son?"

Only a few days before, Meir Amit had met with Moshe Dayan, immediately after his appointment as the new minister of defense. Spread before them was the map of the eastern Negev. They both carefully examined the location where Israel's atomic reactor had been established. Dayan's orders were curt and to the point: "You will have to give this place top priority!"

The defense minister did not have to elaborate in order to impress the importance of the installation on the Mossad chief. The delicate subject of the nuclear reactor and all that it stood for could not be dissociated from the shadow of the Holocaust which had overtaken the Jewish people a quarter of a century before. The slaughter of the six million Jews in Hitler's gas chambers had influenced the thinking of Israelis in peacetime, as well as at the moment when they were again threatened by their enemies with mass slaughter.

In periods of war, the memories of the past and visions of national survival brought a renewed determination: "Never again." Not far from Dimona stand the vast salt pillars of Sodom and Gomorrah, which many insist were formed as a result of some unexplained nuclear explosion thousands of years ago.* The symbolism is plain for all to see. There are those religious extremist Jews who look at Dimona and then cite the story of Samson in the Bible— the same Samson who, when blinded through betrayal,

---

*"Then the Lord rained upon Sodom and upon Gomorrah brimstone and fire from the Lord out of heaven. And he overthrew those cities and all the plain, and all the inhabitants of the cities, and that which grew upon the ground." (Genesis 19:24-25)

brought down the pillars of his prison, destroying himself—but killing all his foes too.

Little wonder that Meir Amit ordered the number of missile batteries around the nuclear reactor doubled. He even drove to the installation with his personal assistant to see with his own eyes that his orders were carried out. Almost overnight yet another electrified system was put up around the location. Yet another mine field was planted between the new fence and the previous outer perimeter, and the defending trenches were deepened.

Meir Amit insisted that Colonel Gideon Eshet take over the role of commander of the missile defenses. He was known to be the best Hawk battery officer in Israel. The military had argued vigorously that he was needed in the front line where "the real fighting was going on," as it was put somewhat forcefully to the Mossad commander. Moshe Dayan intervened in the dispute, and Gideon Eshet was sent to Dimona.

When the reactor's defense system was created, every possible contingency had been anticipated. A highly sophisticated method of defense against a surprise attack by well-trained commandos had been devised and tested again and again. No vehicle or human on foot could get through. There was also a conventional anti-aircraft belt as well as the advanced Hawk missile batteries.

No one, however, had thought of the highly improbable eventuality of an unconscious Israeli pilot sitting in a plane which, by some uncanny stroke of misfortune, would head straight for the silver-domed reactor!

"Of all the damned places in the world where it has to happen, it has to happen here," Meir Amit said to himself for about the twentieth time. The report from air force headquarters left nothing to the imagination. The angle at which the plane was diving toward its destination could not have been more destructive if computers had carefully plotted its course in advance.

They had checked and rechecked. The plane was losing altitude at such a regular pace that unless something unusual happened, or the pilot suddenly recovered consciousness, it was going to crash right into the reactor.

Meir Amit had to act—and act quickly. The responsibility was entirely on his shoulders. He knew all the facts.

There was no skirting the issue, no seeking further information or even praying for a miracle. One word of command from him and the Mystère would be shattered into a thousand fragments. One word and Pilot Yoram would be doomed to instant, violent death.

He knew the young man was mortally wounded anyway. No one would ever criticize him for making that agonizing decision to press the button. Certainly none of the men in the room, watching his every move, would have done anything else. They were all professionals: top men in intelligence, the defense minister's personal assistant, and two of the country's leading atomic scientists. They would respond in exactly the same way that he knew in his heart he had to act. They all knew what was at stake. None of them sought explanations. There was no other solution. They knew it. And he knew it.

Even so, he would have done anything in the world right then to hand over the ultimate responsibility to someone else. Or at least to be able to sit alone for a few seconds and give his order without anyone having to overhear it. In his imagination he mistook the compassion in the eyes of the eight men around him for cold hostility. . . .

Meir Amit had been on many dangerous missions in his life. He had killed men, and his heart had been hardened to the harsh brutalities of life as a soldier and secret service chief. But this was different. To send this youngster, one of the proudest products of the Air Force Training School, to his death was something else. He knew that the horror of blowing up the pilot would rest heavily on his conscience to his dying day.

The red telephone rang for the third time. Colonel Gideon Eshet's voice was frantic. "He's crossing the red line . . . He's now *past* the red line . . . he's diving right on to me . . . Meir . . . I know it's your decision. But it's my responsibility too. I have to press the button."

Lieutenant Daniel Gordon stared with astonishment at his chief. He had served under him for many months. Eshet had always been calm and cool, he was never excited. He never raised his voice. Every single individual in his unit trusted him totally and without reserve.

Now the same man seemed to have lost control of himself. He was behaving in a strange way, as though emotionally supercharged. The lieutenant was quick to grasp that something mysterious lay behind the colonel's unusual behavior. His eyes moved back and forth from the radar screen to his commander. He saw the yellow dot drawing closer and closer. From the scale on the glass radar screen he was able to work out the precise distance the plane was from them, and in which direction it was heading.

Lieutenant Daniel Gordon was very young but extremely talented. He had graduated with honors from the Hawk battery officers' course at an American training camp not far from Washington. He knew his job. He was thus well aware that the "fire" order should have been given long ago. From snatches of conversation that were not really his business, he realized that the dilemma over the approaching plane had something to do with the air force in coordination with the highest command in the land.

Unnoticed, the young officer left his seat, casually moved toward the communication board near the screen, and put on a pair of earphones. He could see the signals, so he was not neglecting his duties. No one noticed him as his finger played lightly with the calibration dial and knobs. He wanted to know what was going on.

The radio sergeant sitting alongside saw what Daniel Gordon was up to but did nothing other than to give him a quick wink. The lieutenant did not need to overhear more than a snippet of conversation to grasp what was happening. A Super-Mystère bearing a Star of David emblem was coming straight for them, an Israeli pilot aboard—perhaps someone he knew personally! Daniel Gordon went pale as he caught the anguished voice of the flight controller still trying to rouse the unconscious pilot.

"Sparrow from Eagle. Sparrow from Eagle . . . Activate your parachute at once! Activate your parachute . . . You are entering the Red Danger Zone . . . I repeat. You are entering the Red Danger Zone . . ."

Ripping off the earphones, the young slenderly built officer took two steps toward his commander. His face was as white as the salt pillars near the Dead Sea. Colonel Eshet did not need more than a glance to understand that what he had feared most was now a reality. The secret he had wanted to keep to himself was now revealed to his own firing officer. He was the last person whom the colonel had wanted to be in the know. Daniel Gordon was the one who had to physically put his finger on the button.

"You can't do it!" the young officer shouted shrilly: "He is one of ours! It's madness! It's the same as murder!!!"

Colonel Gideon Eshet said nothing. He simply raised his powerful forearm and with his open hand clamped his fingers over the young officer's mouth. His other hand rested firmly on Gordon's shoulder. The young man tried to wriggle free. His face turned red with exertion and his eyes darted around in his head wildly like a trapped animal trying to seek freedom.

This was not Eshet's first encounter with the symptoms of hysteria; it arose frequently when inexperienced men suddenly were confronted by the danger of death on the battlefield. He strengthened his grip, holding Daniel Gordon so that he could not move.

His voice was low and gentle, like a father speaking to a distraught child. "Look," he said. "Look at the screen. You can see it. Twenty kilometers away. Nineteen kilometers. Nineteen more kilometers. It is coming straight for us. It does not change direction. You understand what that means? You *know* what it means. It is like a guided missile. It will destroy the reactor. You can see for yourself. You know what the stakes are. You have a job to do. Do it! I trust you."

For a second or two the colonel held the young officer in his viselike grip until he began to feel Gordon's muscles relax. The wild looked drained from his eyes, and in its place appeared shame at losing control. The older man released his subordinate and, speaking softly but firmly, told him to sit down. The lieutenant did as he was told without opposition. There was a deadly silence in the room, for the incident had become the center of attention.

Now the colonel was back in front of the screen. He glanced up through the bulletproof glass of the control room. Every man was alert, near his firing station, ready to take action. The missile launchers were already pointing northeast at the unseen approaching target, as though hungry to thrust out their long fingers of instant death and

destruction. The colonel quietly ordered the standby:
"Prepare for launching!"

Once again he checked to make absolutely sure that the
shift officer maintained the alert from minute to minute at
every firing station. Now all was ready for the final command. For the first time, they were going to fire at a real
hostile target. This was the one that mattered. There
wasn't a man on duty who did not feel his heart pounding
at breakneck speed.

At air force headquarters deep in an underground
bunker, a look of relaxed happiness could be seen on the
faces of most of the NCO's as well as the senior officers.
On the second day of the war it was clear that victory was
assured—thanks to the air force pilots who had destroyed
the planes of their Arab enemies. The huge Russian MIG
armadas of Egypt, Syria, and Iraq, as well as those of the
British-equipped Jordanians, were smashed on the runways
of scores of bases, or else were lying scattered in the desert
where they had been shot down. The pilots were still in
action, but now they were lending close support to the advancing troops and tank columns.

Only the expressions on the faces of the deputy commander and two of his trusted assistants were dark and
morose. Since the late hours of the morning when the
commander of the air force himself, General Mordechai
(Motti) Hod, had been summoned to the general staff
headquarters, the total responsibility rested on the shoulders of his deputy. He was faced with a problem that he
could not solve, no matter how he wrestled and juggled
with all the options open to him. Who in his right mind
could ever believe that one of their Super-Mystères would
be heading like a guided missile, at close to the speed of
sound, straight for the country's nuclear reactor?

He clenched and unclenched his fists. His full, rounded
face was sweating. He knew, and his assistants knew, that
it was a hopeless situation. Finally he picked up the green
telephone and said in a faint and almost inaudible voice:
"He is out of our range. You'll have to take care of him
yourself." He knew what that implied, but he could not
find the words to say what he really meant: "You will
have to shoot him down with a rocket."

At the other end of the line, the chief of the Mossad nodded his head sadly in response to the words of defeat he had just heard. His only reply was simply: "Got it!"

Despite the air-conditioning, the atmosphere in the Hawk bunker command was as heavy and oppressive as the heat outside. Colonel Gideon Eshet did not take his eyes off the yellow dot on the screen. With a quick glance the colonel saw that the young lieutenant was totally in command of himself once more—ready to do his duty.

It was Gordon himself who broke the silence. "They cannot wait more than ten seconds at the maximum. He is approaching absolute minimum range, Colonel."

Eshet nodded in agreement. The jet was not more than three kilometers away. The soldiers could see it with their own eyes coming straight for them with frightening speed in the blue sky.

"Take your seat, son. It's your task."

The moment of hysteria was forgotten, never to be mentioned or even hinted at by either man as long as they knew each other. It was a once-in-a-lifetime incident.

"We are going to bring him down."

The colonel stretched out his hand once more for the red telephone. At precisely that moment, just as his fingers were closing on the receiver, the instrument vibrated with a sharp, grating ring.

"Okay, Gidi," the Mossad chief ordered, "finish the job."

Colonel Gideon Eshet replaced the receiver. His voice was as calm and composed as ever as he called out: "Batteries One and Two. Prepare to fire."

The crew jumped into action. Their bodies reacted mechanically as though wound up by clockwork and then suddenly released.

"On target, sir."

The glitter of the Super-Mystère's wings reflected the sun's rays. It looked beautiful as it came in against the intense blue of the desert sky.

"Range zero, sir."

"Fire!"

Lieutenant Daniel Gordon's face was expressionless as he pressed the button. A column of fire burst upward with a hiss of fearful menace. At first it seemed to travel slowly, then gathered instant momentum. Now the two

19

man-made marvels of technology were approaching each other with a speed nearly double that of sound.

Drawn together as though by invisible threads of total destruction the missile and the plane made contact. No one could tell whether they collided head-on or not. It was too quick for the naked eye to see. Pieces of metal cartwheeled all over the sky. From the control room the flash of light from the explosion looked eerily like a red-hot mushroom.

A split-second later the desert air was as empty and still as though nothing had happened.

Colonel Gideon Eshet lifted the red receiver yet again. "Done," he said and strode from the room back to his private quarters.

For a while the depressed atmosphere in the Mossad command meeting room in the Kirya in Tel Aviv was disturbed only by the puffing sounds of the cigarette smokers. Every man kept his thoughts to himself. There was nothing to say. Even the encouraging reports of ever-fresh victories from the front line did nothing to lift the mood of gloom around the table.

It was Dafna who came to the rescue. She was experienced in such matters. One look at the faces of the gathered group, at her boss whom she knew so well, told her that something dreadful had happened. Dafna had worked in the Mossad nearly from its inception. She knew most of its secrets, she knew the personalities and characters of its leaders, as well as its various agents and operatives. She was a mine of information, and it was fortunate for her country's security that her loyalty and devotion ensured that nothing on this earth would ever induce her to speak.

She brought coffee and fruit juice and plates of sandwiches. With unobtrusive movements she emptied the ashtrays filled to overflowing with stale cigarette butts. She straightened some files on the table and then hurried to the door. She knew that the eyes of every man in the room were following her. She had a special sixth sense, a woman's intuition which always brought her to the meeting room at moments of crisis.

She smiled in such a way that every man in the room

could easily convince himself that her radiance was personally directed at him. In spite of her forty years, she was conscious that she had an attractive figure, and she made the most of it by the way she dressed, for Dafna was well aware of her charms. As she left the room she knew that once again, by deliberately exploiting her femininity, she had succeeded in softening the mood of despondency. She smiled, this time to herself.

Professor Benjamin Bentheim, regarded universally as Israel's senior nuclear scientist, was the first to break the silence. It was fitting that this was so, for he understood better than any of the men in the room the grave crisis which had threatened. His square, strong face reflected the urgency of his words: "We have succeeded in warding off an immediate and unexpected danger to the reactor. Now we have to put our minds to work to find a way of preventing its future total paralysis."

Weighing his words carefully, he added: "If anybody seriously intends to carry out Project 'L' according to the schedule we have established, we must convince General de Gaulle to release the uranium shipment he promised us earlier. After all, he has already received payment! I assume he is the man of honor that he keeps advertising he is, with such haughty pride, in his speeches."

Dryly Meir Amit interrupted: "His honor is such that he will give us back our money—one day. But he will never forgive us for not obeying his instructions. He warned us not to strike at the Arabs, no matter how much they threatened us. We ignored his words of wisdom. That is the ultimate crime in his eyes. I know him well. No pleas, no request, no nice words from us will change his mind. He clearly meant it when he threatened us with a total embargo if we disobeyed him. He will never weaken his resolve."

For a few minutes Meir Amit's grim warning was assimilated by each man in his own way. Some frowned, some muttered under their breaths.

"We will find a way to get uranium."

All eyes turned toward the speaker. It was the first time in the hours' long discussion that he had raised his voice. They all knew him well. They knew that nearly every daring Mossad operation executed far from the shores of Israel had either been carried out by him personally or on his instructions. Very few knew the exact details of these operations, but his reputation was far-reaching.

Michael Binder was officially head of the Mossad's Special Operations Division. He was the most original thinker and daring innovator on the entire staff of the intelligence service. For him there was no problem on earth that did not have some solution. There were those, on the superstitious side, who even suspected that he knew a thing or two about the next life as well.

The deeds and adventures of "Mike"—no one ever called him anything else—had long since become a legend and the subject of countless stories, some true, some imagined. What *was* true was his awesome reputation in almost every intelligence service of the world. His thundering voice and broad shoulders, his handsome features, made him seem too good to be true.

In front of him on the table lay some light brown foolscap files. Mike toyed with them for a few seconds, and then, his voice almost in a whisper so as not to give away any secrets unnecessarily, even in the trusted circle in which he found himself, he said: "Yes, it can be done. I know how."

He stopped talking. Clearly he was not going to explain any further. Across the room General Meir Amit nodded his head. The chief of the Mossad clearly agreed with his operative commander. Mike had envisaged a way of getting the sorely needed uranium for Dimona.

Chapter Two

No one suspected that the small apartment in the poor-looking building with the whitewash peeling from its walls served as Mossad headquarters in an important European capital. It was sparsely furnished with only the barest essentials to give the impression that someone actually lived there.

Sharon Manners sat in the more comfortable of the two chairs. She knew Mike well. After all, he was her boss. And as usual she made no secret of the fact that she found him a fascinating and attractive man. Whenever an assignment was completed and they were in the company of friends, she would frequently say to Mike, "You should apply for the role of James Bond in the movies. You would do it ten times better than the actors they always show on the screen!"

For reasons of his own, which he never explained, Mike preferred the excitement and danger of real-life espionage and secret service work. He lived in a world of shadows and knew that he would never take any bows on a public stage. Yet, despite every precaution, he admitted ruefully in Mossad headquarters that he was a little too famous for his own good. The dossiers on him in such leading intelligence services as the KGB, the CIA, and the French DST were well filled. In all these organizations he had both friends and enemies.

From long experience Sharon knew that she had not been summoned to admire Mike's Nordic good looks. The way he was playing the role of a charming man of the world was her clue that an important mission was in the offing. For ten whole minutes he gave Sharon the impression that he was totally absorbed in her womanly charms. He spoke about music, drama, even the architecture of the city they found themselves in. Sharon smiled at Mike and waited.

Suddenly the timbre of his voice changed. His tone lost the warmth of a man going through the motions of trying to please and impress a female companion. "I need you for a delicate mission," he said abruptly. His eyes were hard now. The caressing smile had vanished.

"I know that you suspect after the success of your last operation in Amsterdam I am always going to use you in the role of a temptress. You are wrong. I don't like doing it. I truly mean that. But there are times when we all have to do things we are unhappy about.

"This time, however, it is not just a question of exterminating a terrorist. This operation is the most important you or I have ever been involved in. I don't exaggerate in the slightest when I say that the very fate of our country hinges on it. I can't go into details now. However, it involves Euratom."

Now the smile was gone from Sharon's face too. She was an experienced agent. Operations involving kidnapping or killing the enemies of her adopted homeland never bothered her. She followed orders happily and felt not the slightest twinge of remorse or conscience about cutting short the life of her "mark." Euratom was something else. It did not require genius to work out that this had something to do with a nuclear operation. She suddenly felt a pang of fear.

As a young girl she had gone on holiday to Japan with her parents. They had visited the Hiroshima museum, and she had been totally unprepared for the horrors on display there. For many years afterward she had nightmares in which she saw the formaldehyde jars filled with floating shapeless pieces of human organs and limbs distorted by the blast of atomic radiation.

There were other sights as well which she could never forget. On the earphones, in English exquisitely spoken by a Japanese translator, it was explained that this object here, or that object there, had been a tree, a pregnant woman, a child. Her shock at the terrifying mutations caused by an atomic explosion and its subsequent radiation had even prompted her to fly to England one Easter to join the tens of thousands of demonstrators taking part in the "Ban-the-bomb" march from the British atomic center at Aldermaston to Trafalgar Square in the heart of London.

Mike seemed to read her thoughts, but he continued as though nothing had happened. "We will have to find out everything we can about the transfer of nuclear material. We already know a great deal about all the key workers at Euratom. Our agents have done good work. You will have to get friendly with one of the top men in the agency. Shortly you will have a dossier on every single one of them.

"However" and he paused for a second—"to be precise, the decision is already made. You can take your pick of three candidates."

Sharon looked at Mike with a slightly sardonic smile. She was strong-willed and highly independent. "I am really grateful to you for being so considerate," she said bitingly. "One out of three. What more could a girl ask for!"

From the desk drawer Mike pulled out three thin folders and handed them to Sharon. She sat back and leafed through them, carefully studying their contents. Each contained a set of photographs, showing head-and-shoulders portraits and profiles as well as full-length shots.

It did not take her long to decide. It was no contest. One of the men was a German about sixty, balding with a double chin and large stomach. The second was a Frenchman, middle-aged, scrawny, and indifferent in appearance. In the third folder appeared a really good-looking male, no more than thirty years of age, she guessed. In typewritten letters beneath his handsome Latin face was the name: "Antonio Bordini. Italian."

Without hesitation, Sharon pushed the open file across

the desk to Mike. "If I have to do what I suspect you intend me to do, then I prefer to work with this one," she said, pointing to the Italian's photograph.

Mike nodded consent. "Okay," he said, "let's go over the details."

Euratom, or to give it its full name, the European Atomic Energy Community, was created by a treaty signed in Rome on March 27, 1957, by Belgium, France, West Germany, Italy, Luxembourg, and The Netherlands to pool their resources and efforts for peaceful nuclear research. The reason they had joined together was that the western European governments finally understood in the late 1950s that if they wanted to stay in the forefront of modern industrial development, they would have to rely more and more on nuclear power.

It was quite simple. There were the superpowers, Russia and the United States. Each had its own program which was aimed at developing nuclear energy sources on an ever-increasing scale. They both possessed vast nuclear armaments.

The rest of the world was now divided into first- and second-class nations; those who had their own nuclear energy powerhouses and research facilities were in the first league, those who did not were merely also-rans. To try and compete with their big brothers in Moscow and Washington the Common Market countries decided to work in harness.

Unlike other Common Market institutions, at Euratom squabbles among members were few and far between. Because there was general agreement on their common interests, the participants gave considerable authority to Euratom. Thus the directors of the organization are empowered to make all decisions regarding nuclear energy production and the manufacture of equipment for reactors. They also concern themselves with the important commercial exploitation of uranium. The board of directors of Euratom are appointed according to a definite political sliding scale. Countries like France, for instance, or Germany, which have advanced nuclear technology, have a large representation. Countries with a small stake in nuclear development, like tiny Luxembourg, have only a minor voice in Euratom. Not very democratic, it is true, but Euratom was created to reflect the harsh realities of life. As one of its founders once said: "We had Stalin in mind when we worked out the constitution. Why Stalin? Because we remembered his comment when asked about his attitude toward the Vatican. 'The Pope?' said Stalin. 'How many tank divisions has he got?' "

Euratom's work is administered by separate executive bodies, which are generally independent of each other. There is the research institution which, as its name implies, plans nuclear research. There is the reactor committee which builds reactor installations. Then there is the supply agency.

This is the most influential and powerful of all three groups. It is in charge, among other things, of organizing uranium shipments to member countries. It has to protect and insure all cargoes of uranium so that they do not fall into unauthorized hands. The supply agency also acts as the purchasing agent for material needed for European nuclear production. It has subcontractors all over the globe, and its director is a powerful man indeed, with a heavy responsibility to match his status.

Antonio Bordini was the right-hand man of the director of the Euratom supply agency. There had been murmurs of protest when he was appointed. He was not only very opinionated but, even worse, he was "not serious," as one or two of the senior members in the organization had complained. This might, however, have something to do with that most unlovely of human emotions—plain jealousy.

True, Bordini was good-looking and vain. He flirted— highly successfully—with every woman, married or single, in the building. But there was no question of his qualifications. He was a brilliant scientist whose technical grasp of nuclear physics and of the commercial and industrial exploitation of nuclear energy was second to none. He was a world authority, and that was why he had been given the job.

Antonio Bordini parked his new Alfa-Romeo carefully in its numbered place on the lot near the building which housed the offices of Euratom's supply agency. A speck of

27

black dirt on the gleaming roof of his brand-new car made him frown. From a side pocket in the door he took a yellow cloth kept expressly for this purpose. He rubbed away the offending stain, and then with his handkerchief gave the area an extra little polish.

He surveyed his new toy proudly. Then, with a careless gesture, he replaced the handkerchief in the breast pocket of his English-style tailored jacket and hurried through the heavy glass door of the headquarters.

He really looked the typical Latin lover conventionally portrayed in the movies and so eagerly sought after by young female tourists to Italy every summer. Perhaps his only defect was that he was a little on the skinny side, as Sharon was quick to notice when she saw him in the flesh for the first time. He had worked very hard as a student at the Sorbonne in Paris, then in graduate studies at a university in the United States, too hard probably to waste his time on playing sports or taking daily exercise.

His thinness clearly did not inhibit the natural exuberance of the Italian. After waving to the security officer, who first recognized and then welcomed him immediately with a salute, Bordini blew a kiss at the receptionist and gave a dazzling smile to a middle-aged woman waiting for the elevator. It arrived on the ground floor at the precise moment that he reached for the button.

"Ah, it seems to be my day," he said with a little smile of indulgent self-satisfaction to the small crowd now getting into the elevator.

A mere five minutes after Antonio's tall figure disappeared behind the glass doors of the agency, a small red Renault drove into the parking lot. No one paid much attention as the French car cruised slowly around the area, apparently seeking a suitable resting place. Finally it pulled up gently alongside the spotlessly clean Alfa-Romeo.

The girl sitting in the driver's seat checked her eyeshadow in the mirror; it was the only makeup she wore. On the seat alongside her was a careless pile of the better fashion and women's interest magazines. Three 35-millimeter cameras, a Pentax, a Nikon, and a slightly battered Leica fitted with a telescopic lens, lay on the floor. In the back was a large black box filled with film, filters, odd lenses, and flash equipment.

The girl seemed in no particular hurry. Thoughtfully she combed her long, jet-black hair. She touched up her eye makeup once more. She locked the rear doors, made sure that the passenger door was also secured, and then slid deftly out of the driver's seat. Carefully she checked to see that this, too, was locked. There was several thousand dollars worth of equipment lying casually about in the car.

She was tall and slender and smartly dressed in a chiffon blouse that subtly outlined her firm and prominent breasts. She wore Gucci shoes and a handbag to match, and her large sunglasses were perched on top of her head. She was the prototype of the successful professional woman. She strode out of the exit of the parking lot casually, as though she had done it a hundred times. No one challenged her.

Fifteen minutes later she was back in her seat. She checked her face once more in the mirror, then started up the engine. The car reversed in a wide semicircle, then stopped. Instead of moving forward, it suddenly reversed powerfully to the sound of a heavy whine from its accelerator. With a crunch of grinding metal, the rear bumper of the Renault tore into the side of the blue Alfa-Romeo.

The sound of a car accident is guaranteed to attract a crowd of curious spectators. Today was no exception. Within a few seconds several dozen passersby from the adjoining street were staring at the badly damaged Italian car, and someone commented: "What do you expect from a woman driver?"

From his protected cubicle, the parking lot attendant came running. He had been dozing. Who was this unauthorized woman who had crashed into one of the directors' cars? He was worried. There was going to be trouble and he feared it could cost him his well-paid job.

The attendant glared at Sharon Manners who was standing by the badly dented door of the Alfa-Romeo and looking distraught. *"Pardon. Pardon . . ."* she kept saying in French to no one in particular. "I just don't know how it happened." She spoke with a strong American accent, there was no mistaking that. To the angry, gesticulating attendant, she had simply repeated her stock phrase: *"Pardon ... pardon."*

The attendant rushed off to get Antonio Bordini in person. He had wanted to call from the security desk, but the man in charge strongly advised him to go upstairs and break the bad news in person.

Bordini did not know it yet, but he was about to get a rude shock. He had spotted the car attendant standing at the door of his office, nervously clasping and unclasping his uniform cap in his hands, and he signaled to him to hang on until he finished his telephone call. The attendant was kept waiting for nearly ten minutes, for Bordini was busy talking to the head of a large energy institution in Washington. There was no question of interrupting the conversation.

Down in the parking lot Sharon went to her car and from her crocodile handbag took a pen and pad of paper. In large, clear script she scrawled her apartment telephone number and underneath, in smaller writing, added:

> "Please forgive me for hitting your car. It was entirely my fault. If you will call my number I will arrange compensation for the damage caused to your car through my stupidity. In the meantime please accept my deepest apologies.
>
> Sharon"

Tearing the sheet of paper from the pad, she walked quickly over to the damaged Alfa-Romeo. At first she ignored the somewhat ribald remarks of the remaining male spectators. Then losing control for a fraction of a second, she muttered under her breath in English: "Male chauvinist pigs!"

She gave a quick professional look at the rear of her car, "her battering ram" as she later described it to Mike, and smiled to herself. Thanks to the thick protective bar, which protruded almost a foot above the bumper, her car was unscathed; she drove off with a squeal of tires.

Her rapid departure had nothing to do with the jeers of the bystanders. Sharon was worried about the imminent arrival of the car's owner, for she had spotted the car attendant go off to call him to the scene of the accident. She had to be gone before the Italian arrived.

Antonio Bordini was still on the phone. In front of him was a list of orders for uranium shipments destined to be delivered to various European nuclear reactor research stations.

"Yes. Yes. Yes," the car attendant heard him say over the telephone. "The next consignment of the yellowcake you need from the United States will not arrive for another three days . . . I tell you that is sure, I have been on the phone to Washington. By the way, sorry to keep you waiting on the line, I was talking direct to the United States . . . Yes, to Hamburg as previously arranged . . . To be absolutely sure, let us say five days; we still have to unload; and there's customs and so on." There was no doubt about it; the Italian was highly efficient at his job. It was a heavy responsibility, being in charge of nuclear fuel shipments, both processed and nonprocessed. He had to ensure that all of the European community's nuclear reactors, and the industrial concerns involved with the exploitation of the material, got everything they needed.

Those critics who said he was too young for the job had to admit—grudgingly perhaps, but admit nonetheless—that he worked with American-style efficiency. Antonio Bordini had been looking forward to his lunch with the German delegate. He enjoyed his highly paid job, and he also delighted in the aura of success that surrounded it. As a perk he had a brand-new car every year (within a budget limit which he was trying to get raised—he had his eye on a blood-red Ferrari for the following year). There were lavish expense account lunches, as well as membership in exclusive private clubs, which meant so much in that most snobbish of cities. His wardrobe was extensive and costly, a necessary prop for the endless cocktail parties and the series of beautiful women who passed in and out of his life.

Now suddenly, with the attendant's announcement, everything had gone sour. Antonio Bordini was like a spoiled child. His critics would have been gratified to see him behaving like a raving lunatic beside his damaged car. "Only an unbalanced, psychologically unstable personality

31

could get so excited about a car" would have been the disapproving reation of certain of the senior members at Euratom.

Cursing loudly in Italian, he literally stamped his elegant, beautifully polished brown shoe on the ground. Suddenly he noticed the note stuck under his windshield wiper. The delicate perfume tickled his nostrils as he grabbed the paper in his right hand. "Jicky," he thought. He was a true Latin lover. He could tell immediately what kind of girl he was dealing with by the brand of perfume she used. Carefully he read the round, feminine handwriting. Suddenly his temper cooled. He had been making a fool of himself. He was covered by insurance anyway— paid for by Euratom. The driver of the vehicle that had damaged his car was clearly an elegant lady. She was proposing compensation. She was apologizing. She had left her phone number to make amends.

Maybe it *was* his day after all.

He went off to have lunch. His anger was appeased by an excellent meal, a magnificent bottle of Bordeaux—and the delicious thought of that intriguing telephone number. . . .

Sharon was busy shampooing her hair when the phone rang. It was five minutes past seven. She wrapped a large bath towel around her head and hurried to the bedside table where the instrument was ringing away. Drying her hair with her left hand, she picked up the receiver.

The voice at the other end was totally unfamiliar to her. The man spoke excellent French, but with a foreign accent. Sharon picked out the Italian intonation almost immediately. She was cold and distant as Bordini toyed with her in his best playboy style.

"It's Antonio," he said jocularly.

"Antonio?"

"You don't know any Antonios? Ah, I can see you have never really lived!"

Sharon pretended to be slow to hang up as she answered with a hint of anger: "I think you are making a mistake. I really don't have time to play games. Good————"

The Italian cut in abruptly: "Let me give you a clue. Let us say we have already run into each other, in a manner of speaking, although we have never met. Your name is Sharon, is it not? You did not declare the rest of it in the little love letter you left me!"

His voice rang with laughter. This was a deliberate ploy. How many girls had told him how beautifully he laughed; so musical, "so sexy," as the English wife of a colleague had whispered to him once when her husband had been sent on a trip to Frankfurt by Bordini himself.

Now Sharon was apologetic. She was filled with remorse and embarrassment. She was even careful to stutter as she said: "I promise that I will reimburse you for all the damage I did to your car. I really am so sorry. I thought I was in first gear and instead I was in reverse. I just don't know what happened to me. If you just tell me where to send the check, I'll do so as soon as you send me a bill for the damages."

Antonio Bordini rose to the occasion magnificently. "If I were a louse I would take your money," he said. "But I am not. I'm fully insured. And what's more, I am absolutely thrilled to know that there are still honest and sincere people in the world. There are so few who would have bothered to leave their name and address after such an incident."

He paused for a second, then added: "But I can tell from your voice that you are a stranger here. I *am* going to demand some compensation. I insist that you come and have a drink with me at my club so that I can see who it was that wrecked my lovely car."

Sharon sounded relieved but remained cautious. She also knew the rules of the game. "I don't really want to put you to any trouble . . ."

The tone of hesitation in her voice reflected the first "no" of the virtuous woman who is not going to give in easily. "Actually I am on assignment here and am rather busy."

Bordini now poured on the charm. His voice deepened as he deliberately injected a note of masculine authority into the conversation. "Well, either you compensate me or you don't! And I refuse to take your money!"

Sharon gave in. "All right," she said with a little laugh. "But not at any private club. I have heard some strange things about such places—or so my mother warned me!"

They both laughed. The ice was broken. The date was fixed for 6:30 the next evening at the Café Bruxelles. Bordini said he would be carrying a brown attaché case. Sharon was to wear a white blouse and black skirt.

"He really is good-looking," she thought to herself as she saw him approach through the crowd of men and women enjoying their evening aperitifs. If this was to go the way she realized it would surely have to, then at least she would not need to close her eyes and think of something else.

The conversation was trite and superficial. As brilliant a scientist as he was, Antonio Bordini obviously regarded this bad driver as just another easy victim to be led sheeplike to his bed as quickly as possible. Sharon realized she would have to shake him up, or give him a powerful shock early on. As yet she was not quite sure how. She listened to his mechanically trotted-out banter and silly jokes. She smiled discreetly. She was restrained but not unencouraging.

The couple became friendly enough for a light kiss as they parted that evening. Firmly but politely, Sharon declined the invitation for a drink in Bordini's apartment, but without any hesitation she accepted his suggestion for a late lunch the next day. They arranged to meet in front of the Euratom building at 2:00 P.M.

As the young woman entered her apartment she glanced around quickly to make sure that nothing had been moved, indicating a break-in. Carefully she lifted the edge of the wall-to-wall carpet in each room. There was no sign of footprints in the white powder sprinkled in key areas. Her expensive Japanese stereo system was in the same state of carefully staged disarray as when she had left the apartment earlier in the day.

Everything in the tastefully decorated apartment was in order. There were two Cézanne silk-screen reproductions on one wall and a Japanese poster on another; elsewhere the walls were decorated with framed photographs neatly clipped from magazines like *Vogue* and *Marie Claire*. "This is my own work," she would proudly point out to visitors who asked what sort of things she did as a fashion photographer.

Kicking off her shoes, Sharon dropped into a deep armchair upholstered in white imitation sheepskin. She reached for the telephone receiver on the low mustard-colored console beside her and made a long distance call to Paris.

The masculine voice that answered was low and cautious. "Arthur speaking," it announced.

"I owe you an apology," said Sharon in flawless French. "I had an accident, which explains why I am late in getting in touch with you . . . Nothing serious. I was not hurt or anything like that . . . The driver happened to be a rather nice Italian who accepted it all in good spirits. He even took me for a drink! He insisted on inviting me to lunch tomorrow——"

Arthur cut her short. His voice was urgent and pressing. "Come to the point!"

"Sorry," Sharon replied, "I know you have problems with the printers and that the deadline has been brought forward."

Arthur again broke in: "I've discovered that another magazine is after the same thing. We really have to beat them to it. Otherwise the whole project will be wrecked. I need all the pictures I can get, but I need them fast! The story has to appear in the next issue, otherwise we are all in serious trouble!"

The girl could hear the almost desperate note of urgency that had crept into "Arthur's" voice. She had never heard him speak in this vein before. It must be tremendously important. It was impossible to mistake the way he had underlined the words "serious trouble."

He broke into her thoughts: "Forget about any other articles we are working on. Forget about any of the pictures we discussed. You will have to pull out all the stops—all of them!"

Sharon arrived at the front of the Euratom building at precisely 1:45 P.M. She checked the time on the tiny silver watch on her wrist. Carefully, she took up a position where she could see the elevator doors without attracting undue attention to herself.

For eight minutes she watched the way the arrow-shaped floor indicators lit up. Each elevator had its own independent system. At the precise moment when three of the arrows lit up simultaneously she dashed forward. She had been hoping for all four, but time was pressing. Three elevators arriving on the ground floor level at the same time would have to do. Pushing open the glass door to the entrance she moved quickly toward the elevators now emptying out passengers. She did not run but took quick, determined steps. She smiled confidently at the elderly security guard—a smile of friendly recognition.

His reactions were slow. Before he could move out of his seat and take the few steps toward the elevators, she was mingling with the waiting crowd. He called to her, but she pretended not to hear. Angrily he strode toward the elevators, but by now Sharon was in one of them, squeezed toward the back. The door closed smoothly, and the elevator moved upward.

"Madame! Madame!" the worried security guard called after her. He knew that the regulations were strict. No one without an identification tag prominently displayed was allowed past his desk. Visitors had to be specially cleared via a complicated checking system.

Not one of the dozen men and women in the elevator took the slightest notice of "Madame." No one even seemed to notice that she was not wearing the compulsory identity tag. The elderly bald man who was pressed against her was not in the slightest suspicious when she asked him, "I have forgotten—what floor is Signor Bordini working on? It's slipped my mind!"

"Antonio Bordini?" he asked. "The fifth floor. Room 504." He was so embarrassed by the bold smile which was directed straight into his eyes that he looked down toward the floor of the elevator in total confusion. It had been a long time since an attractive girl had flashed him such a provocative look.

Sharon got out of the elevator on the fifth floor, and, without the slightest hesitation, marched boldly into Room 504, after a perfunctory knock on the frosted glass door. She swept into the room like a hurricane.

Antonio Bordini was flustered—and astonished. Frantically he covered the sheets of paper in front of him. Then, anxious not to give the impression to his visitor that he distrusted her and was trying to hide something, he casually placed them into a folder. He was at a loss for words.

His comparative youth and inexperience now counted against him. He just did not know how to handle this delicate situation. The girl was not supposed to be there. How had she penetrated the building's security system? How had she found his office?

For the first time, he realized how truly lovely she was. He had been enchanted when he had first cast eyes on her the previous day. Now, despite his intense embarrassment, he suddenly found his breath was caught in his throat. This girl was really registering on his emotions.

"How did you get in?" he half pleaded, trying to rebuke her for her unexpected arrival and, at the same time, not wanting to sound hostile.

Instead of a reply, she unleashed her most dazzling smile at him and said simply: "I got tired of waiting!" Sharon could play the game as well as he.

He tried to find words to explain that he would be in dreadful trouble if she was found in his room in top-secret Euratom! But that would have meant that he was subordinate to others. His Italian pride forbade his admitting this. So, with a little forced smile, he remarked mildly: "In the general interest it would have been better if you had asked for me downstairs."

With a laugh she responded: "You forget that I am a photographer for magazines—I am used to getting to see people without bothering about silly rules and regulations." Then she added almost coyly: "Perhaps you want me to go . . . ?"

He leaped up. "No, of course not," he said, worried that she would just walk out again. "But would you mind if I just finish some work I have? Then we can go and have lunch." He had intended to usher her out of the office, somewhere, anywhere. There would be a devil of a row if she were found with him. He knew he had enemies in the building who were only too ready to exploit such a situation to the full.

"That's all right," Sharon said, and without further ado, she sat down in an armchair in the corner and picked up a magazine from a glass-topped table. On its cover was a nuclear-powered generating station. She flicked through its pages as though she found it the most fascinating subject in the world.

She crossed her legs carefully and discreetly smoothed the pleats of her dress. A nicely cut slit ran from the knee halfway up her thigh. Her tanned legs showed through the gap, just as she knew they would. She had no need to look at Bordini. She was well aware that he was staring at her legs while pretending to gather up his papers. He was so flustered that he did not notice that her trained eye was taking in every detail of his office: where papers were stored, which cupboards were closed with heavy locks, which were open and contained unimportant items like stationery and reference books. The position of the desk, the window, Bordini's private telephone number on the instrument at his side were all stored away in her memory.

She did not have long to wait for her lunch. With an impatient flourish Bordini piled up all his documents and with one hand pushed them into a steel cabinet on his right, then locked it.

"This is not going to work," he said. "You're filling the entire room with your presence—and your perfume. I can't stand it a second longer—not on an empty stomach anyway." He had recovered his composure at last and was once again the smooth playboy. She returned his smile and stood up.

They left the building together through the door leading to the courtyard. He was cautious and canny now. "This way will be preferable to a frontal skirmish with the security man. He will never believe that you are my long-lost sister from Milan!"

Chapter Three

At first glance the place looks like a school building, or even an oddly shaped factory. Certainly it does not seem in the slightest bit sinister or secretive, planted as it is in an outlying suburb of Tel Aviv.

On closer examination it is clear that there is something unusual about the establishment. It is surrounded by three barbed-wire fences strung among the trees and bushes in such a way that they are not really visible unless one looks hard and carefully. Two of the fences carry 400 volts of electricity. One tall, domed concrete building is larger than the surrounding smaller, square-shaped structures. These in turn are ringed by well-tended bushes and flowerbeds. This is one of the most closely guarded establishments in the country. Most of the Israelis who pass by almost daily are quite unaware that it is the headquarters of the secret service organization.

The tall, blond, athletic figure who drove up to the outer entrance in his American Buick was not asked to produce his identification credentials. He was recognized immediately. At both the second and third gates, the armed guards also greeted him warmly: "*Shalom. Shalom,*" and signaled him to drive right through. There was no one in that intelligence community, right down to the newest recruit, who did not know and recognize Mike on sight.

In all honesty, very few really knew just what his job was. Either you were in the know, or else you kept quiet. That was one of the first things you were taught—never to ask questions about personnel who work alongside you. You might guess—but in the long run it was better that you remained in ignorance.

It was no secret, however, that Mike really did belong to the very highest echelon of the organization. He *looked* like the popular image of the secret service agent. He was tall, with blue eyes, and had a powerful personality. He was used to giving orders, and he led other men as naturally as if he had been born to it. He had one other priceless asset. He was lucky. He never banked on his good fortune, but during moments of true crisis, when he was really up against it, lady luck had always remembered him and come to his rescue.

Mike was commander of the Special Operations Division of the Mossad. This agency is in charge of all security and espionage matters outside the boundaries of the country. It is so secret that newspapers in Israel are not even allowed to mention its leader's name. At the time, the man in charge was General Meir Amit. He commanded not only Mike's specialized group but also a research department, an Arab affairs unit, and a foreign relations desk.

The "intelligence community," as it is referred to, includes within its ranks other sections besides the Mossad. There is the Shin-Beth, which concerns itself with protecting internal security and carries out counterespionage duties within the boundaries of Israel. The military intelligence wing has its own command structure and, as its name implies, concentrates on gathering material concerning the armies of the surrounding Arab states. Recently, it has had to involve itself with Soviet naval penetration of the eastern Mediterranean. The police force also has an intelligence group—the MTM, which is chiefly involved with measures against Arab terrorists within the boundaries of the state.

It is the Mossad that is the most powerful section of the intelligence community, and in the Mossad the most glamorous unit is the Special Operations Division, commanded by Mike. This group is responsible for the spectacular coups that make newspaper headlines the world over. Sometimes this is resented by the "back-room boys" at headquarters, and jealousies have been known to sour relations.

Mike was a true professional, one of the finest operating anywhere in the world. He had proved it again and again, whether in assassinating a terrorist, kidnapping a man who was needed for "discussions," or penetrating into the most difficult of hostile environments. Mike had no equal. Yet, when persuaded to talk, he was the first to pay homage to the one individual, Isser Harel—or "Little Isser" as he was known because of his small physical size—who had built the Mossad from scratch into one of the universally recognized first-class intelligence agencies.

Mike had fought in the War of Independence of 1948 when Israel had to cope with the combined invading armies of its Arab neighbors to assure itself of a place in the sun as country in its own right. Earlier, Mike had been an officer in the British army, but in 1949, despite being a "winner," he felt embittered.

"I was about to go drastically wrong," he admitted with candor to his closest friends. "I was thinking of making a career of crime and becoming a gangster. After all, I had the right training for it. I just could not fit into civilian life. Isser drafted me from the army and asked me to serve under him as an intelligence officer. It was the greatest service any man had done me in my life."

Now he is on the "wanted" lists of more than fifty countries. Yet he has never been caught. He operates to this day. He has always insisted on leading from the front, going out in person to conduct the most hazardous operation. He is a master of disguise. He is also a man of the greatest cunning and resourcefulness—a talent which only emerges when the going gets tough.

Mike was now in charge of one of the most complex and difficult missions of his life. He had to get his hands on a shipment of uranium. Uranium. The life blood of a reactor—the nuclear reactor at Dimona. He had had long experience in other espionage activities and was convinced that he had done it all. Now, he admitted, here was something completely new. He knew nothing about uranium or how reactors worked, or even where it was that you got your hands on the material.

Hence his hurried steps in the direction of the research department of the Mossad. The key to his past success lay in careful preparation. He never went out on a mission, nor sent his men to carry out an assignment, without first studying every possible detail of the matter at hand. Mike knew that he could get total and complete information on anything he wanted.

The research division was filled with some of the leading scientific and technical brains in the country. Right from the beginning in the early 1950s, Isser Harel had insisted that only highly skilled men and women could serve in the intelligence community. Even if information was not known at headquarters, there was not a single professor, university lecturer, or other learned individual in the entire land who was not ready to pass on his knowledge to the Mossad.

The area of research covered by the department spanned five continents and 120 countries. The division gathered information from behind the Iron Curtain by means known only to itself. For instance, it was this unit that had been the first to obtain a copy of the minutes of the twentieth annual communist party convention meeting in Moscow. This was the historic gathering at which Khrushchev made his famous speech that destroyed Stalin's image as the great idol of the Soviet people.

It is the research department that maintains close contact with the equivalent divisions of the French, German, and other Western intelligence communities, including the CIA. Mike knew that he would not only get theoretical help from the "wise men," as he called them; he could also count on their sympathies, for many of those with advanced degrees at the university level had had actual field experience in the countries in which they specialize. They knew what a man who had to go out into "the cold" faced.

Mike also liked to look at past operations in the area that was under his focus at any given time. Not only did this help him "steal" good ideas used in the past, but he could also spot the mistakes that had cropped up too. In addition, he found that reading how other agents had operated sparked his own vivid imagination.

Oddly enough, he was a little disappointed at first when shown the "sea missions" section. Then, on a dusty cardboard folder, he noticed a handwritten title that immediately caught his attention: *"Operation Sea Thief 1948."* A theft on the ocean waves. Just what he was looking for!

Mike smiled to himself as he glanced at the careful way a diligent operative had written out the story of the *Lino* in laborious longhand. In those early days the Mossad was such a rudimentary organization that it did not even employ a secretary. Agents had to do their own administrative work. Clearly this particular "pirate" had never learned to use a typewriter.

Mike read fast. Like every member of the unit, he had undergone a speed-reading course to master the art of taking in whole paragraphs instead of going through line by line. "Operation Sea Thief" had been a daring coup. Primitive—but daring.

Mike frowned at some of the elementary blunders committed by the squad as the story unraveled. "They took too long," he muttered half aloud. "They were clumsy and undisciplined." But he read on. Somehow his sixth sense told him that the key to getting his hands on the uranium he wanted for his country lay somewhere, somehow in a sea hijack.

In 1948, Mossad espionage agents had "received information" that a 450-ton ship, the *Lino,* was carrying in its hold 8,000 guns, 8,000,000 rounds of ammunition, and other military hardware including cases of hand grenades. It had sailed from Fiume in Yugoslavia and was heading for Beirut.

The weapons supplied by the Czech government were destined for Syria to be used by the Arabs who were then preparing for a Jihad, a "Holy War" against the yet unborn Jewish state. While sailing in the Adriatic, the *Lino* sprang a leak. The engine room was flooded and she was forced to limp to the port of Molfetta, not far from Bari in southern Italy. A Mossad squad of several men and a woman was instructed to sink the ship there.

Mike blinked hard in surprise when he saw that the

code name of the girl involved also happened to be Sharon.

The present Sharon's predecessor had played an important role in the operation. The "action" was launched at the harbor after the squad had traveled there to survey the area. Two of the agents had slid into the sea with a primitive bomb made of TNT and some rusty parts from an abandoned motorbike. The bomb, carefully wrapped in waterproof material, was strapped to the back of one of the agents. The swimmers had to make their way past a British warship as well as Italian patrol boats on the alert for any such attack. The *Lino* was blown up; it went to the bottom of the harbor with all its arms hidden under a thin layer of onions taken aboard at Fiume as camouflage.

With the help of British experts (the Labour party was then under the sway of a powerful pro-Arab policy), the cargo was salvaged. Most of it was found to be intact and in perfect condition. Now a head-on clash developed between the intelligence services of several countries, each striving to get its hands on the weapons. There were violent confrontations in Italy between communists and right-wing elements who accused each other of bringing the arms to Molfetta in order to wage civil war.

Sharon, the Mossad agent, now reverted to her role as "Geri Pelma," a Yugoslav refugee who worked as a newspaperwoman in Rome. Once again, Mike was struck by the similarities between his own female agent, Sharon Masters, whom he had decided to use in order to get his hands on a supply of uranium, and the girl in "Operation Sea Thief."

Like his own Sharon, who was at that very moment making eyes at an Italian scientist, Geri Pelma was strikingly beautiful and quite ready to utilize to maximum effect the gifts nature had showered on her. The Yugoslav woman had made it her business to be known to every diplomat of importance in the Italian capital. The city was a vital base at the time, for a large majority of the illegal immigrants challenging the British blockade off the Palestinian coast boarded their rusty old ships in Italian ports.

Obeying instructions, Geri Pelma promptly seduced a new arrival in Rome, Major Fuad Mardam-Bey, a cousin of the Syrian prime minister. Fuad had been sent to Europe to insure that the salvaged arms were brought back to his homeland. The major was soon hopelessly in love with the journalist. He told her all his plans for outwitting the enemy, the Jews, and he also ran up enormous bills keeping up with her astonishingly expensive tastes. He was totally enraptured by her. Kind friends of Geri's lent him money to help out. The Syrian was now well and truly trapped.

He was "advised" to charter a new vessel, the *Argiro,* which his pals found for him, since he had so little time to handle such details himself. Geri had made it her business to keep him occupied night and day in her Roman apartment. Major Fuad was warned that "Israeli spies" were everywhere in the city; he must not breathe a word about the *Argiro* to a soul.

So it was that neither British intelligence agents nor Arab spies had any inkling of the *Argiro*'s purpose or destination when she slipped out of port one night. The Syrian was equally ignorant of the fact that two Mossad agents had been hired as "engineers" to join the all-Italian crew. Just prior to departure, Major Fuad had bought more arms from funds sent from Damascus. They too had been loaded onto the *Argiro.*

A few miles from shore, a fishing boat signaled the ship to stop. Two men climbed aboard and explained that they were Egyptian security men sent to guard the vessel. They informed the captain that instead of heading for Beirut, they would now sail for Alexandria. When the skipper protested mildly, the Egyptians produced revolvers they happened to be carrying. The *Argiro* changed course.

As a large welcoming party headed by Major Fuad waited in Alexandria for the ship's arrival, the two mechanics and the "Egyptians" seized the vessel. The Arab leaders grew alarmed when the *Argiro* failed to arrive and Fuad was sent to Rome to find out what had happened.

Geri welcomed the Syrian major with open arms. She persuaded him that it would be politically "immature" to appeal to the Italian authorities for aid. For the next two days she helped him forget his problems as they dallied in her apartment. Three days later, the *Argiro* arrived in Haifa.

In order not to provoke a diplomatic incident with the

government in Rome, the entire crew was taken to Kibbutz Bet Oren on Mount Carmel and given a free seven-month holiday. Their only restriction was that they were not allowed to leave their "vacation camp." Their baffled relatives received postcards from all over the globe saying that they were safe and well.

Finally the Israeli police "discovered" the kidnapped Italians and liberated them. The angry authorities in Rome were promised that the criminals involved would be punished as soon as they had been found, but somehow the matter got lost in an administrative muddle.

Major Fuad was put on trial in Damascus for treason. Only his powerful family connections saved him from the gallows. Instead, he was given a life sentence. The major wrote many letters to Geri Pelma at her address in Rome. He never got a reply. No one in the Italian capital ever again saw or heard of the Yugoslav newspaperwoman.

Mike smiled at the amateurish way in which the operation had been carried out. But it *had* been successful. The arms coming at the height of the war between Israel and the surrounding Arab states was a godsend to the beleaguered little country. For a full thirty minutes the Mossad Special Operations Division chief made careful notes in a child's orange exercise book. "Operation Sea Thief 1948" was going to be his model for a far more dangerous venture involving much higher stakes—fuel for an atomic reactor.

For the next nine hours Mike kept the research staff hopping from one set of shelves to another. He wanted to know everything he could about uranium: its sources, which companies mined it, and what shipping lines transported the raw and then the processed material all over the globe. He then made his way to the Mossad's foreign relations department.

It was now well past midnight, but the caller wanted all available information immediately regarding nuclear installations in countries where Israeli embassies or consulates were to be found. Only a skeleton staff was on duty, but he insisted that key personnel be dragged out of their beds to speed up the information-gathering process.

There was some grumbling at the way interdepartmental toes were being trodden on, but Mike was totally unmoved. He demanded instant cooperation with peremptory curtness. This was no time to be polite, or to "go through the right channels in the morning," as one outraged clerk was rash enough to express it before he felt the rough edge of Mike's tongue.

The commander of the Special Operations Division had to put together in a ridiculously short time an operation whose feasibility seemed doubtful to even the most optimistic. He *had* to get around the embargo imposed by the president of France and obtain the uranium Israel so urgently needed.

Next day Mike had the outlines of his plan ready. He drove in his Buick to a nondescript building, and again three sets of security officers at the triple row of barriers waved him past with nothing more than a nod and shouted greetings of "*Shalom. Shalom.*"

For several minutes he watched a dozen trainees—nine men and three women—being coached on how to wire up explosives in the most effective way to booby-trap a car. These apprentice agents were graduates of the most elite unit in all of Israel. They belonged to a band of operatives who carry out daring and spectacular operations—many of which have made headline news all round the world, from the kidnapping of Adolf Eichmann in the Argentine in 1960 to preparing the ground for the rescue of the hostages held at the Entebbe airport in Uganda by a joint band of German and Palestinian terrorists in 1976.

Recruits undergo a sixteen-month training program. Only a small percentage survive its grueling schedule. On several occasions the head of the Mossad, Meir Amit, had complained to Mike that his expectations regarding future agents were too high.

"The more discipline, the more pressure they survive in training, the more they can be relied upon in field operations," Mike insisted. "I know what I am talking about. I have been through it all personally."

Again and again he said: "My operatives must be the best professionals in the world. We don't have the resources other countries possess, so we have to make up in quality what we don't have in quantity. My boys and girls have to be the nearest flesh and blood can get to being superhuman."

He laid down the basic rules. Agents had to be able to speak several languages fluently. They had to know all about explosives and how to handle a whole range of weapons. They had to be crack shots. They were compelled to be experts at killing with knives as well as with bare hands. They had to be masters of disguise, and it was essential for them to be able to stand up to torture without breaking. The sixteen-month period of demanding training developed every one of these qualifications.

With the help of a psychologist at Tel Aviv University, Dr. Shuval, Mike devised a novel memory-training technique which produced the most outstanding results. Every single recruit who graduated in his section was capable of memorizing in seconds the entire contents of letters and documents, lists of names or numbers, as well as taking in the concise details of photographs, and then accurately repeating them many hours later.

Mike also insisted on a fanatical level of physical fitness for his recruits. His training program called for more than mere theoretical mastery of every subject in the art of espionage. Agents were given orders to penetrate heavily guarded bases, either working individually or as a team.

On more than one occasion, a trainee had been caught and shot without warning. This aroused considerable controversy, for it was felt that it was unnecessary as well as being an immoral practice to waste precious lives.

Mike refused to be moved. "They know the dangers," he retorted with brutal realism. "Any recruit can withdraw or resign at any time—and no bad feelings. But if they are going to be caught right here in Israel, then they would never survive working in a totally hostile environment anyway." Many of the trainees stumbled and fell along the way.

During their training they were sent out on "apprentice missions" to Europe and even behind the Iron Curtain. The recruits were constantly kept on the move. Even during hard-earned rest periods, when the most dedicated of "new boys" felt they had earned the right to a breather, they were rudely wakened and sent out on a totally unexpected exercise or mission which frequently seemed to have little sense or purpose.

Nothing was neglected. Even such minute details as how to behave when going through passport controls in different countries or how to smuggle dangerous items like chemicals for explosives and weapons through the most stringent customs controls were carefully explained, and practiced again and again.

Only when all these stages, testing physical and mental toughness, were successfully mastered did candidates face the most dreaded of all obstacles, the "torture barrier." Trainees were aware of what lay ahead of them. Frequently, however, they were led to believe that they had truly fallen into the hands of genuine enemy agents. While on a mock mission, for instance, the apprentice would suddenly find himself abducted by unknown individuals on a dark street corner or when returning to a hotel room late at night. The operative would be unceremoniously dumped into the back seat of the trunk of a car at gun point.

Taken to a dismal-looking room with no windows in an unknown place, the agent would be given the full treatment of degrading and painful torture. He or she would be tested to the limit of endurance; frequently they would lose consciousness only to find more excruciating tortures facing them on recovery. It was only after this ordeal of fire by torture that the apprentice became a full-fledged agent.

But no agent who went through this harsh survival course ever feared to take calculated risks on the ground that he might crack under torture if caught. He *knew* what pain during intensive interrogation meant. Thus every individual in Mike's crack unit went into action with total self-assurance that he could handle any and every situation in enemy captivity.

Mike had crystallized his philosophy: "My operatives must feel that they are capable of standing anything, that they can do anything we ask them to do without the slightest hesitation or remorse." To critics of his system, he responded with the reply: "I have never asked any of my men to do anything that I myself have not personally experienced or carried out."

Now he stood patiently waiting for the sabotage lesson on the booby-trapped car to be completed. Then he strode over to the instructor and said: "Can you spare me a minute?"

He did not wait for a reply. The instructor knew it was an order despite the polite turn of phrase. As the men walked away, Mike placed an arm around his companion's broad, muscular shoulders. The instructor was dark-skinned, of slightly less than medium height, with a thick head of curly black hair.

"I want to take you back to your seafaring days," said his boss. "You are going to become a qualified sailor again. You know, working with cables, ropes, knots, anchors, navigation charts, all that kind of thing."

Meir Azoulai smiled. He often felt more at home on the high seas than he did on dry land. After he had done his national service he volunteered for a stint of several years as a professional in a naval commando unit. For a while he had been attached to marine intelligence, and it was in this capacity that he had sailed on merchant ships as a second mate.

"I'll have to brush up my knowledge on which are the best red-light districts wherever it is we are going," he said with a laugh.

"There's not going to be any time for that sort of thing," replied Mike unsmilingly.

An instinct warned Meir Azoulai that his boss was deeply worried. Normally he would have joked right back, for he had an awesome reputation of being a lady's man without scruples.

Meir asked no questions. Just as he taught his apprentice agents to obey blindly without argument, so he automatically let his chief understand by his silence that he was ready—yet again—to do whatever was asked of him.

It was a golden rule in the Special Operations Division that the price of refusal, or the slightest sign of trying to evade a duty, no matter how disagreeable, boring, or apparently futile, would result in an immediate grade "N" rating. That meant only one thing—instant dismissal without appeal.

"I'll have Shauli Mizrachi from the Arab affairs department join you tomorrow. That's when you start."

Shauli was a graduate of a special reconnaissance unit. His dedication and professional skills, combined with his

Yemenite origins and the darkness of his skin, made him a prime choice for assignments in the surrounding Middle Eastern countries. He could speak half a dozen Arab dialects and he understood the Arab mentality perfectly. He looked like an Arab—as, indeed, did so many agents in his division.

He had already played an important part in a number of highly successful operations. One of them succeeded in planting a Mossad agent, Eli Cohen, in Damascus, where he became an important government official; he was being groomed for defense minister until he was revealed as a spy. Shauli's other exploits had been crowned with equally impressive results but were not publicly known for the very good reason that nobody had been caught.

As so often in the past, Mike again turned to the same group of dark-skinned men to participate in a combined operation. Shauli Mizrachi had already been ordered to present himself within a few hours. Like everyone else in the unit, he was ready for duty, anywhere, at any time.

"In the meantime you had better get back to your apprentices," Mike ordered Meir Azoulai. "They look to me as though they need some sharpening up. Discipline looks slack."

Meir Azoulai had never known his boss to be so edgy before. This was clearly going to be one hell of an operation. . . .

Chapter Four

Professor Benjamin Bentheim was obviously struggling.

"We are dealing with isotopes," he said. "Most of the naturally occurring ones and all the man-made ones have unstable nuclei and as a result they are throwing off charged particles spontaneously. This is known as radioactivity. Now, uranium compounds emit rays continuously and these can penetrate solid materials. I should, however, add that the isotopes of a particular element are distinguished from each other by the structure of the nucleus and not by their chemical properties."

The professor, one of the world's most famous nuclear scientists, was standing in his spacious study in the single-story office building near the silver dome of the nuclear reactor at Dimona. Before him a solitary pupil was seated, a pupil who had suddenly arrived out of the blue, without an appointment, and had asked politely but firmly: "Can you please tell me all there is to know about uranium, atomic energy, the theory and practice of nuclear fission, the operation of reactors, and any allied information. I can give you two hours."

For one wild moment the scientist had a vision of Rubinstein being asked to teach a young man who could not even read music, how to play the piano and reach virtuoso levels in one sitting. But the professor was well aware of the importance of Mike's mission, and he was trying his best.

Mike had already collected as much research material as he could. Now he sat making diligent notes in his bright orange exercise book.

"I will try and use simple, unscientific language," the professor said to Mike. "I am sure my colleagues would be a bit shocked, but the terms I use will be comprehensible to the layman."

Mike nodded. "I won't give you away to your colleagues," he said solemnly.

"Let us go right on to uranium," the professor resumed. "Ninety-nine point three percent of the uranium in nature exists in the form of the isotope U-238, so numbered because it has 146 neutrons and 92 protons. This is the normal form of uranium. However, point seven percent of uranium exists as U-235, which has 143 neutrons and 92 protons. It is this rare form of uranium that interests us. And the reason is its three-neutron deficit. The nucleus of U-235 seeks to achieve internal balance by acquiring the three neutrons it lacks.

"Therefore, if you bombard the outer wall of the U-235 nucleus with a neutron, it ruptures the wall relatively easily and penetrates the nucleus. The energy released when this happens is enormous. It can, in fact, be calculated without much difficulty according to Einstein's formula: energy equals mass multiplied by the speed of light squared."

The professor paused. For a second or two he thought back to the days when he had his first lecture in elementary physics. His teacher was a fierce man who would stop abruptly every now and then to grill an inattentive pupil with sardonic comments just to make sure he was absorbing the words of wisdom. The scientist looked at Mike and thought better of trying to trap him.

"If you recall that the speed of light I have just referred to in the Einstein formula is roughly 300,000 kilometers per second, and you square it, you begin to grasp the size of the force involved. Just think of ordinary energy. The process of exploding one gram of uranium 235 releases energy equal to 23,000 kilowatt hours of heat. Or put more simply: it is equivalent to the release in a fraction of a second of all the energy contained in three tons of coal or a large number of barrels of gasoline. If all the atoms in one kilogram of uranium underwent fission, the energy released would equal that released by burning three million kilograms of coal."

Now well in his stride the scientist went on: "The process I have outlined is called enrichment. But of course there is an alternative way of producing energy from uranium on a similar level. That is by bombarding uranium 238 with an additional neutron. This creates an unstable isotope. Adding the neutron converts the uranium into uranium U-238 V, which is an isotope with different properties. This isotope is called plutonium. All you need is a lump the size of a tennis ball to make a bomb. The material is unstable because the extra neutron wishes to escape. Here too the bursting of the nuclear wall and the release of the neutron creates tremendous energy."

"This uranium we need," Mike burst in suddenly. "What does it actually look like?"

Bentheim looked at his pupil with a pained expression on his face. He found it hard to grasp the total ignorance of this man. He might have an awe-inspiring reputation as a spy, but hadn't he gone to school? The professor rubbed his head, which, to Mike, bore a remarkable resemblance to the silver dome outside, and cleared his throat. "Well. In nature, uranium is found in the form of a yellowish brown ore. Nobody bothered much with it until the brilliant Italian scientist Enrico Fermi made an important find. But I ought to explain. The binding energy of a uranium nucleus 238 is very great. If the nucleus can be partly disintegrated, enormous energy is produced. Now Fermi . . ." His voice trailed off.

Then with a flash of inspiration he saw how to bring home the parallel to the secret service man clearly more at home with guns than with physics.

"Fermi discovered that if you fire neutrons at atomic nuclei as you fire bullets from a pistol, you release nuclear energy. The trouble was that in the early stages he only managed to release a small amount of energy. It was then discovered that if you fired at a *heavy* nucleus like uranium, breaking it up into two large nuclei, you got nuclear fission. Under careful control the fission of millions of uranium atoms in a chain reaction will result in the release of an enormous amount of energy in a short time.

"Oddly enough," the professor added, "Fermi's discovery was the first confirmation of Einstein's theory of energy, which holds that each atom has within it energy tens of times greater than any that had been produced up to that time.

"All that remained was for technical solutions to be found to a known problem. We have seen the results for ourselves. For instance, the bomb that was dropped on Hiroshima used uranium 235 fuel; in the second, on Nagasaki, it was plutonium. The success of these two atom bombs in mid-1945 brought about an immediate rise in the price of uranium. The ore was then seen to be of tremendous importance. All information on its sources and production became state secrets all over the globe."

Mike already knew this. Entire regions where this radioactive mineral was found, in countries like Rumania, Czechoslovakia, northern Canada, and the western regions of South Africa, had been declared restricted zones, barred to foreigners and closely guarded.

"Do you know where these quarries or mines are—precisely?"

The professor looked at Mike thoughtfully: "I realize what you are thinking. I know the location of every source, both major and minor. But you are wasting your time in this direction. Control of these sources is total and absolute. The regions are usually extremely isolated. Euratom, the Americans, the Chinese, the Russians—they are the sole masters of these sources.

"The uranium ore that is brought out of the earth is usually called 'yellowcake.' It has to be refined to convert it into uranium metal. Weapons grade fuel is obtained by using natural uranium in a reactor designed to yield the highest possible proportion of plutonium as a by-product of the process of fission."

Bentheim looked out of the window at the silver dome. When he turned back to Mike, his face was grave and troubled.

For three and a half hours Mike listened carefully to the professor. At the end of this time Benjamin Bentheim was decidedly impressed. He was pleased both with himself and his pupil, who had now grasped every piece of information he was going to need for his venture.

The Mossad man understood why it was so important to get the uranium the scientists at Dimona needed. The professor had made him party to some startling state secrets, for he knew that this information was safer with Mike than with any other man in all of Israel.

As they shook hands on parting, the scientist said: "Even if you cannot cope yet with a full-length Beethoven sonata, you can at least manage a Strauss waltz."

Seeing Mike's puzzled look, the professor added hastily, "Never mind. Just a little private joke that would be appreciated only by my good friend Rubinstein."

The look of solemnity returned to his face as he continued: "Just concentrate on getting the uranium. I must have it. The lives of every man, woman, and child in this country may depend on it."

Chapter Five

Sharon was sitting up in bed. She looked around her, pleased with the way she had decorated the room. Everything was in blue—blue sheets, blue pillowcase, blue bedspread, blue paper on the walls. The Picasso and Braque prints all had blue as their dominant color.

Antonio Bordini returned to her bedside. He was wearing a black and red silk bathrobe. Sharon's first reaction when she glanced up at him was how magnificently handsome he was. This was the third time in her career as an operative that she had been compelled to use her feminine charms on an assignment, but this was the first occasion that she had experienced a feeling of conscience about the matter, as she later admitted to Mike.

Antonio had set out to impress this woman who had dropped so by accident into his life. Now he was playing the role of the perfect gentleman. He was the one who had gotten out of bed, who made the coffee and rang the porter downstairs to send up the Sunday papers.

It was the 22nd of October, 1968.

As he skimmed the headlines, Bordini suddenly exclaimed: "What a rotten business!" He showed Sharon an article describing for the first time the inside story of how

57

an Egyptian torpedo boat had sunk the Israel flagship *Eilat* with a Soviet missile the previous October. Sixty sailors had died in the attack.

"What's so rotten about it?" Sharon replied, her mind on needle-sharp alert. "They are always killing each other, aren't they?"

Bordini was on the defensive. "I don't particularly like Jews," he said. "I keep meeting their scientists—there are a lot in my profession, you know. They think they know it all, if that's what you mean. But at the same time I get enraged when I see injustice. I'm talking about racial injustice. I knew some Kurds when I was at the university and I was horrified by the way they were treated in their homeland by the Arabs. It puts me in a fury to see people tyrannized simply because they're a particular color or religion.

"I probably sound like a soft-headed liberal; actually I'm nothing of the kind. In fact, I'm very conservative. But I don't like the way blacks are treated in South Africa. I was horrified by what happened to the Jews under Hitler, and I don't like the way their little country is threatened now by millions upon millions of Arabs and the whole might of the Soviet Union."

The Italian stopped suddenly; he looked—and felt—embarrassed at the emotionality of his outburst. But Sharon drew him out. "I can see you are a man of great sensitivity in every way." She smiled at him. Antonio seemed to grow two inches taller; her compliment had touched his Latin pride.

He confided to Sharon that it was the Six-Day War of 1967 that had suddenly focused his attention on the Middle East. Like so many other non-Jews, he had been visibly impressed by the spirit of the Israeli airmen and soldiers who had swept back the overwhelmingly superior armed forces of Egypt, Syria, and Jordan in a spectacular victory that had no parallel in modern warfare. Not being a man who did things by halves, he had decided to find out all he could about Israel; he read books on the slaughter of the Jews in Nazi Germany, the birth of Zionism, and how the modern state of Israel had been created in a little more than half a century from the barren waste that was then Palestine.

Whenever the subject of politics came up in conversations in the corridors of Euratom, Bordini had made no secret of where his sympathies lay. It was, therefore, no accident that he was on the Mossad's list of prospective candidates for Sharon. The Israeli intelligence service always knew the background and viewpoint of key personnel in any organization it was trying to penetrate.

This kind of investigation was one of their tested methods and was conducted in a very scientific way. Would-be victims were graded according to a "desirable objectives" scale. The Italian had emerged very high on the list, and Mike was delighted with Sharon's choice—even though her motivation was not quite the same as his.

Sharon listened carefully. It was the moment to bait the trap.

"Come to think of it, you do have a point about Israel," she said casually, not interrupting her companion, but waiting for the moment when he paused to drink his now half-cold coffee. She told him about a few professional assignments she had been sent on to Israel. The desert had provided her with beautiful backdrops for some of her most successful photographs. Finally she confided: "You know, I had a very good friend who was an Israeli. Actually he was a pilot. He was killed in a raid over Damascus in the very war you have just mentioned."

Bordini was a sensitive and warm-hearted man. He was quick to spot from his companion's tone of voice that the "friend" had been more than just another acquaintance. He was not in the slightest jealous; rather, he suddenly felt a wave of sympathy for Sharon. She in turn now sensed that his unexpected gentleness toward her was genuine and not part of his carefully cultivated "lover" technique. She confessed that she was quite ready to "do many things for the people of Israel," although she herself was an American.

The Italian was pensive. "Actually what they really need is not new tanks or better guns. All that is primitive. I know what I am talking about. What they really need are a few nuclear bombs. Also nuclear tactical weapons. Believe you me, there is nothing better designed to dissuade would-be aggressors than the knowledge that the foe is nuclear-armed—and even more important is ready to use the full arsenal in the interests of national survival. As the matter of fact, I happen to know that they are sniffing around. I've heard it myself from our security people. They are actually so worried they are tightening things up."

Sharon now decided to launch a full-scale shock attack, the way an artillery commander suddenly opens fire with every big gun at his disposal.

"Actually you can do more than talk and show sympathy. You can help them. If I understand your job correctly, you are responsible for the movement of nuclear material to and throughout Europe. I am certain they would pay you well for the information you have at your command. And I'll tell you something else."

She paused for a second or two. "I am pretty certain they know what to do with the material."

Antonio Bordini was startled. Sharon could see his jaw muscles tighten. A look of suspicion appeared in his eyes. Instinctively he moved away from her.

She burst out laughing. "I am playing at being a spy," she joked.

Antonio Bordini relaxed and joined in the laughter. The suspicion that had disturbed him a few seconds ago had totally evaporated. Sharon did not mention the subject again. Instead she asked to see the fashion pages of the Sunday papers and studied them professionally for several minutes.

That evening as they dined in one of the city's most expensive restaurants, Sharon could see that her companion was not quite himself. He was pensive, as though weighing a difficult problem. She excused herself and from a public phone near the ladies room put through a long distance call. The conversation was one-sided, brief, and to the point.

"I now have the picture session lined up," she said crisply and lowered the receiver. No one could accuse Sharon Manners of squandering the Mossad's money. She smiled serenely as she rejoined her companion at their table.

The Israeli merchant marine ship *Mazal* was a two-hour sail from its destination, the Mexican port of Vera Cruz. Suddenly the radio operator burst into the command bridge through the door of the map room. The ship's captain stood near the radar unit and gazed at the Gulf of Mexico shoreline that was clearly painted on the bright screen in front of him.

The captain, who was about forty, had an unusually smooth, almost babyish face not often seen in senior naval officers. The only clue to his real age lay in the uneven creases around his eyes and in his graying hair.

At first the crew had been very worried when they were told that their next commander was going to be Captain Ze'ev Biran. It was no secret that half his life had been spent in the security services and that he had played an important role in many of the Mossad's most daring exploits. He had also served as second-in-command of a destroyer until he was charged with setting up a submarine combat unit. Ever since Israel had been established as an independent state in 1948 he had taken part in every secret intelligence mission at sea involving his branch of the armed services. He had taken a variety of vessels to areas considered "impossible" to penetrate, and on several occasions had landed strike units in hostile areas, later recovering the commandos in stormy seas and under enemy fire.

In particular, Captain Ze'ev Biran had an unequaled talent for navigating dark, rock-strewn inlets and coves where no skipper in his right mind would ever dream of taking a ship. Again and again the Mossad had called on his expertise to rescue an undercover agent who was trapped or who had to escape quickly with documents or microfilm.

Then suddenly Ze'ev Biran had quit the intelligence service. It was thought he had finally broken under the strain, that a life of constant tension and dicing with death had become too much for him to bear. He declined to discuss his reasons, and no one pressed him for an explanation, for there is a tradition in the Israeli intelligence service that any man can quit whenever he likes, with no bad feelings on either side.

Ze'ev Biran had joined the merchant fleet. His love for the sea was such that he could not envisage any other kind of life for himself. He passed his captain's examinations, and he made it clear that he was quite happy with the prospect of spending the rest of his days on the command deck of a cargo ship sailing from one port to another in regular shipping lanes.

The apprehension of the crew of the *Mazal* when they heard of his appointment was understandable. The reputation of Captain Ze'ev Biran was such that they were convinced their lives would no longer be worth living. They feared that their new commander would rule them with a rod of iron.

However, he quickly put the crew at ease. He was astonishingly lenient; even the humblest deckhand was free to chat with the skipper about any subject under the sun. Regulations were overlooked and rules bent to make everyone's life as agreeable as possible. But despite Biran's amiable exterior, there was not a man on the *Mazal* who did not sense that beneath that baby face was a will of steel, and that, when and if necessary, the fiercest discipline would in a fraction of a second sweep away his friendliness. Nothing was said, but captain and crew quickly understood each other. As a result it was a happy ship.

Now the radio operator came running as fast as his legs could carry him. He had sensed that the message he was carrying was urgent, and he was not going to risk being the first to experience the rough edge of Biran's tongue.

At first the skipper was as calm as ever as he stretched out his hand to take the decoded radio communication. It was doubtless a routine notification from the shipping agent regarding a change in sailing schedule or ultimate destination. As Biran's eyes skimmed over the message, the radio operator saw his face turn white. He bit his lip in an unconscious gesture of sudden anger. The fist holding the telegram clenched and unclenched, then tightened again until the knuckles stood out like four angry bubbles trying to burst their way through the taut, stretched skin. Captain Ze'ev Biran did not have to look twice at the signature of the sender. It was Mike's code name.

"Awaiting you at the pier. Return home. Instructions on the way."

Two eyes, hard and cold, seemed to bore their way right into the brain of the radioman. "I would like to send a reply immediately," Biran said. "The message reads: 'Get off my back. Edward.' "

The captain knew that by uncovering his code name quite openly he was committing an unpardonable breach of security, but he was too angry to contain himself. The startled second mate standing next to him heard him mutter: "I don't give a damn!"

Minutes later when he calmed down, the skipper realized that his gesture had been stupid—as well as futile. Mike would not be put off. Nothing put Mike off. He was a human bulldozer who crushed all opposition in his path with utter ruthlessness. Therefore, Captain Biran felt no surprise when he spotted a Mossad man waiting for him on the quay before the first rope had snaked its way between ship and shore. Although he did not know the agent's true name, he remembered him from two or three occasions in the past.

"That bastard Mike," he thought; "he didn't lose a second. He just took no notice of my reply." Biran felt a surge of fresh anger as well as bitterness at the way he was being taken for granted. For he knew in his heart of hearts that no matter how much he objected he would finally be forced to submit to the will of the sender of the telegram. "It is not a question of neglecting my duty to my country," he told Mike later stormily. "It's a matter of principle! I am a free man!"

The short, stockily built Mossad agent climbed aboard. They greeted each other, but Ze'ev Biran refused to shake the offered hand. As they went down into the cabin, the skipper studiously ignored the agent. He was deliberately rude. He signed the custom authority's papers and those of the health officials. The Mexican officials were invited to have a drink. So was the insurance representative.

Unflustered, the operative simply sat in a corner without saying a word. Biran knew he had been sent by Mike. He also knew that the agent would sit it out for Eternity if necessary. Anything, no matter what, was preferable to returning empty-handed to the Mossad chief of the Special Operations Division. The Mossad agent waited patiently, taking no notice of the official proceedings and the exaggerated and prolonged hospitality that was being offered to the Mexicans.

Finally the two men were alone. The short man came straight to the point. "Mike sent me. He wants you to come to our office on shore to exchange a few words."

The pent-up frustration and rage burning in the breast of the *Mazal*'s captain exploded in one violent outburst. "I asked Mike to leave me alone. I am no longer interested in his games. No more. Tell him to go to . . ." His voice trailed away.

The Mossad agent's eyes had not left Ze'ev Biran's face for a second. "Listen," he said. "Don't take it out on me. Just do me a personal favor, will you? Please give him your answer yourself."

Despite his outburst, which he now felt a little ashamed of, Ze'ev Biran found himself smiling. He knew exactly how the man in front of him felt. "Okay," he replied affably. "I'll tell him personally."

"And a lot of good it will do me," he thought to himself.

The Israeli "representation" in Vera Cruz was nothing more than a lawyer's office in a faded white brick building. A name plate "Migal and Salomon" indicated that it provided commercial services for various Israeli enterprises in the port.

Captain Biran and his companion entered the large air-conditioned office through aluminum-trimmed doors. A young man seated at a heavy wooden desk got up the moment the pair entered, as though obeying previous instructions. Mike's messenger, who had reminded the skipper that his name was Yehoshua, picked up the receiver but had to wait ten minutes before getting a line to Tel Aviv. Within seconds a secretary had responded to the code word by promptly putting the call directly through to Mike's desk.

Yehoshua handed over the receiver with a sigh of relief. "He's all yours. You can speak quite freely."

The cheerful voice of the driving force behind Special Operations cut the captain off before the first words even began to form on his tongue.

"Hello, Ze'ev, you toothless old sea-wolf! Don't you think it's time you did something useful for a change?"

Ze'ev Biran interrupted. "Listen," he shouted. "Don't

you understand? I said leave me alone, and I meant leave me alone. I am not interested! And that is all I am saying!"

It was Mike's turn to break in. He was businesslike and seemed quite untroubled by the irritation and rudeness of Biran. "It will be a quick business. I promise you that. Then you will be able to get back to your dreary job of being a bus driver at sea before you've even had time to get nostalgic about other more exciting things."

Knowing that shouting or dishing out insults would have no effect whatsoever, the captain tried to use reason and logic. One after another, his arguments were demolished or simply ignored. As a last resort he even pleaded: "I am too old for this sort of thing now. I'm not the man I used to be. You know that."

The Mossad commander was cold now and his voice was filled with reproach: "You really will age quickly if you keep on pouring quantities of whisky down your throat as if there were no tomorrow. Just as you did in Rosalie's Bar in Houston last week."

How did Mike know about the incident in Rosalie's? He would have been ready to swear that there had been no one in that bar who could have identified him. Mike had hit him where it hurt most, in a very vulnerable spot. His voice filled with suppressed rage, the captain replied: "All right. We will sort that out in a month's time when I dock in Haifa. That will be number one priority on the agenda."

This was Captain Ze'ev Biran at his most dangerous. But again it was Mike who held the whip hand: "Sorry, friend. You come on the first El Al flight via Mexico City. And that is tonight. Your ticket is ready for you."

"It can't be done," Captain Biran protested. "Even you can't arrange for a ten-thousand-ton vessel to sail without its captain."

Mike laughed at Ze'ev's discomfort. "Don't worry. Your replacement is already in the air. He'll be landing at Vera Cruz Airport about one and a half hours from now."

The line went dead.

That night Captain Ze'ev Biran caught the plane as arranged in Mexico City. He never even saw who his replacement was.

Only a few minutes elapsed before the telephone on the desk of the Special Operations Division was in action again. This time the call was put through to the secretary's room of the agricultural machinery production plant at Kibbutz Givat-Brenner.

The voice of the caller was curt and brooked no questioning.

"But the man you want is right now underneath the engine of a combine-harvester at the other end of the building . . ." protested the secretary's assistant. "Can you please try later . . ."

"I will wait until he's finished," said the caller. "Then tell him to come straight to the phone."

Reuven—known to everyone as Ruby—Goldman dried his hands on a piece of cotton waste. His face and overalls were streaked with oil and grease. His spiky hair, which he had once described as "putting barbed wire to shame," lay thickly over his scalp. A tall and muscular man, he had dark brown eyes that were constantly darting around, giving him the appearance of an alert mole.

He wiped his hands again before taking the telephone receiver. The voice at the other end was unmistakable. He would have recognized it immediately even in a crowded room with dozens of others talking at the same time. No one who had ever worked under Mike's direct command could forget his voice.

"Ruby," the voice all the way from Tel Aviv thundered amiably into Goldman's ear. "How are you? Do you think you can find me a little corner when I stay at your place next Friday night? . . . No. Alone. I won't be any trouble . . . Why should you be so surprised that I will be coming on my own? Sometimes a man wants to be on his own, to smell a little fresh country air. Is there a law against it?"

Ruby was on his guard. Every nerve in his body warned him of trouble. Whenever Mike was casually friendly, there was something desperately dangerous in the offing. From experience he knew that Mike never took holidays. He never slept alone either, if he could help it. And he had never expressed a wish before to smell clean "country air," as he termed it. Something really big was up.

Ruby was cautious, but he also wanted Mike to know that he was not fooled for a second: "Listen, will you forgive me if I tell you that I don't believe a word of what you've just said?"

The laugh exploded in his ear. "Well, believe whatever you want to believe. I'll see you Friday evening. *Shalom.*"

The line, like that to Vera Cruz, went dead abruptly.

Chapter Six

Friday night.

For over an hour Ruby argued that he had done his share—more than his share—in carrying out dangerous missions. He had retired from the intelligence service. He was middle-aged now and he wanted to enjoy his life working with machines on Kibbutz Givat-Brenner.

"You keep appealing to my patriotism," he said. "You *know* I am a patriot. But there are other patriots besides me. As a matter of fact, I can recommend some individuals who are dying to prove themselves . . ."

Mike was unmoved by the plea that the master mechanic wanted to be left in peace. "The destiny of the country may be at stake," he argued.

"The destiny of our country is at stake every day, sometimes three times a day," said Goldman dryly.

"You'll have to believe me when I tell you that I really do need you," the Mossad commander persisted. "I came to you because you are the best. And you know I am not a flatterer. You are the only man capable of carrying out this mission. I cannot tell you any more about it right now. But I tell you what I will do. Agree in principle. Then later, when I *do* give you the details of what has to be done, if you can provide a better name than your own, I will agree to release you and take him in your place. I give you my word. I can't be fairer than that, can I?"

The wall of resistance was crumbling fast. Ruby was beginning to feel the flow of adrenaline and a sharp tingle of excitement. "And what about the kibbutz? I can't just shove off without any explanation or reason why I must leave my work."

Mike patted his shoulder as he got up: "No problem. My secretary will be working on it within the hour. By morning there will be a formal application stating all the arguments. They will be convincing, I can guarantee that."

Mike got up. It was five minutes past eleven. "I did want to spend the night," he said, "but I have to be back in Tel Aviv shortly after midnight." He shook hands with Ruby, and without another word he was gone.

Benny Arnheim was so intent on the mass of wires and tubes he was working on that he did not even hear the prolonged ringing of his doorbell. The radio room was large. Strange machines and apparatus bristling with knobs and aerials occupied almost every square inch of the shelves and lay littered all over the floor. There were metal trays on which rested lamps, cables, and reflecting dials.

Despite the apparent chaos, the room was immaculately clean, in contrast to the neglected bedroom and living room piled with clothing, sheets, and blankets as well as other personal possessions. Benny's friends sometimes chided him for "living like a wild animal." He looked puzzled when they criticized his personal habits and would point to his radio instruments and say proudly: "You won't find a speck of dust there. Everything is in its place."

He was a sworn bachelor. Ever hopeful, his friends had introduced him to girls, for he was not an unattractive man. Somehow none of these encounters ever came to anything. "The trouble is," said his friends sadly shaking their heads, "the only thing he lives for is his radio equipment. He is married to it."

This was almost literally true. Benny Arnheim regarded any activity that was not connected with radio equipment and its operation as little more than a waste of time. Even the books and magazines he read were concerned with the one subject that he loved with a single-minded passion. He was fascinated by any kind of instrument that served to relay information and that presented a face of dials and knobs you could turn.

Nothing pleased him more than to be summoned to the home of colleagues who had problems with their radios or hi-fi systems. Benny's eyes would light up and he would tinker for hours, taking everything apart into minute pieces and then putting them together again. Sometimes he made improvements that would have surprised even the manufacturers of the equipment. For not only was he a man who could repair radio equipment and coax life back into damaged items, but he was also an inventor and innovator. His particular joy was to improve existing equipment and dream up completely new instruments.

Several of the most important parts of the Mossad's central short-wave transmitter in Tel Aviv had been based on his own ideas and developments. This powerful instrument was capable of reaching every corner of the globe. It had ingenious scramblers built into it which made the conversations transmitted to agents unintelligible, unless they, in turn, used special gadgets which were totally Benny's brain-child.

Mike rang the front doorbell repeatedly He knew the radio man was inside, but with a shrug of his shoulders guessed that Benny was so absorbed in his work that he was oblivious to the sound of the ringing.

After a quick look around to ensure that he was not being watched, he removed a weird-looking instrument from his pocket and eased the tool into the lock. In seconds, the door was open. Silently he crossed the neglected living room and entered the holy of holies—the radio den, as Benny called it.

For a full two minutes he stood there, silently watching Benny at work. It's a good thing I am not after his blood, the Mossad commander said to himself. He gave no sign whatsoever that he was there.

When he finally spoke, he was standing a mere two feet behind the radio fanatic. Benny leaped into the air as though he had been stung by a swarm of bees in a delicate part of his anatomy. In one hand he held what looked like

70

a soldering iron and in the other some wires he was joining to a switch on the central platform.

"You should be glad it was me and not some other
people I could mention," said Mike with a laugh.

Benny ignored the remark and replied in his normal,
slow, calm voice: "I've got to find the bastard, Mike. The
short-circuit must be in here somewhere inside this coil of
wires." With a small screwdriver he pointed to a coil of
yellow, brown, and red wires, none of which was more
than a fraction of an inch in diameter.

The Mossad commander could not help but smile at this
dedication to the task at hand. But he had urgent business
to transact. "That bastard will have to wait a while,
Benny," he said. "Sitting in my office are the equipment
and new instruments which arrived this morning, according
to the specifications you drew up. I'd like you to come and
service them and make sure everything is functioning. I'll
see you there in two hours. And while you're about it,
warn your central transmitting people that they will have
to manage without your expertise for a little while. We are
leaving in a few days' time. Make sure you call in the
passport office on your way to my office. You'll find some
interesting items there for you."

Benny had wanted to complete the work he had been
engaged in all day, but Mike was already heading for the
apartment door. Knowing he had no options, Benny went
to pack.

Gad Ullman was a civil servant. He was a senior man
and highly paid. The income tax inspector who checked
his returns each year, and who knew more about Gad's
private affairs than did his own wife, was totally unaware,
however, that this small, skinny, and rather insignificant-
looking individual had another profession in life.

Gad Ullman was a killer. An exterminator. And what is
more, he loved his job. He looked forward eagerly to every mission proposed by Mike. His face would light up
whenever he heard the Special Operations commander
over the phone. Only with the greatest self-control could
he prevent his trigger finger from getting itchy and start
rehearsing yet again that smooth, gentle, and caressing

pressure that singles out the master marksman from just another good, competent sniper.

Gad Ullman was extraordinarily thin. His wrists and ankles were slender, his face delicate, and his hair as fine as silk. "Fragile" was the adjective that immediately came to mind when trying to describe his dominant characteristic.

In all honesty he admitted that he had never dreamed of being involved with guns or the art of sniping. He had never handled any weapon before being called up to do his national service. He had not looked forward to being a soldier. People always stared at his thin body when he got undressed, and as a child other boys had poked fun at his slight frame.

On his first morning at the training camp his sole ambition was to find a quiet spot for himself somewhere and keep out of everyone's way. Gad Ullman was not the stuff heroes are made of. He knew it, and it did not particularly bother him.

For a short while, the civil servant now turned reluctant soldier did manage to mind his own business. Then one morning he was taken to the firing range. A rifle was thrust into his hands and suddenly he found himself the center of attention.

The instructor simply could not believe his eyes. "Ullman, are you sure you have never shot before? You are not lying to me, are you?"

Defensively Gad responded: "What am I doing wrong? I really am trying my best!"

It just so happened that Gad was a natural sharpshooter. He was even more amazed than the other recruits. Promptly assigned to the general staff reconnaissance unit, Ullman quickly justified the faith his shooting-range instructor had shown in him, proving the instructor's proud claim that he could spot a potential crack shot almost from the moment he fired his first bullet at the distant target. From that moment ten years earlier, Gad had found his niche in life.

He was frequently "lent" to Mike's Special Operations Division, and whenever anyone had to be killed quickly, silently, and efficiently, Gad Ullman, the Exterminator, was summoned from his desk in the civil service. Not even his family had the faintest inkling of what it was he did when he went on trips "connected with administration conferences."

Gad Ullman had taken part in many spectacular operations, some publicized and some totally secret. Mike regarded him as a true artist in the business of killing. Whether the target was a Nazi who had escaped justice, a terrorist who needed to be put out of action permanently, or any other enemy of his people, Gad was the man for the job. He could use any known weapon with unrivaled virtuosity. He had his own private arms collection, from a miniature revolver that could be hidden in the palm of one hand to an antitank missile launcher needed for a "kill" against a large object which had to be blown up. The Exterminator's tools were kept at Mossad headquarters in the Kirya.

One of the secrets of his success was that he trained regularly. Either on his way to work, or during his lunch hour, he would take a little trip to the shooting range, pick a weapon, and put in half an hour's practice. His record impressed even Mike—with good reason. For Gad Ullman had never been known to miss his mark. It was not this, however, that gave the marksman his greatest sense of self-satisfaction—not even the proud boast of his colleagues that he was the best sniper in Israel, or anywhere else, they would claim, but rather the knowledge that he had never needed more than a single shot to kill his enemy.

Being a deadly marksman was not the only factor that counted in the civil servant's favor. In appearance, he looked so innocent and insignificant that no one ever suspected him of being a secret service agent. In addition, his temperament was so perfect that if a computer had been fed with all the information and data needed for a successful undercover exterminator, it could not have found a finer specimen than Gad Ullman.

He was always calm and cool, even in the tightest corner. On the practice range, where marksmen concentrate totally on what they are about to do and then carefully aim and shoot, he appeared to be quietly meditating, almost in repose. Bullets might be flying in all directions, bombs might be exploding; he might have been cramped up for hours in a cupboard or been hidden for days in a dark room; whatever the circumstances, Gad Ullman was never flustered or discomforted. When he took aim and fired, it was as though he were protected in his own serene cocoon.

None of his fellow agents would ever forget the way he had shot an ex-S.S. officer who had carried out particularly horrible experiments on concentration camp victims during the war. A fight was going on at the time, and the former Nazi was struggling fiercely. The man had raised his revolver in the midst of a crowd of agents and had aimed straight at the Exterminator. It was as far as he got. A single shot right to the middle of the forehead, as though the point of impact had been carefully marked out beforehand with a compass, brought the mission to an abrupt and dramatic end.

When Mike telephoned, Gad Ullman was dictating a letter to his secretary concerning new building regulations for agricultural structures for the storage of vegetables.

"I want to see you," said the chief of the Special Operations Division. "In about an hour."

Gad Ullman finished his letter. His secretary did not notice the sudden glint in her boss's eye. Then, minutes later, he was no longer at his desk.

Chapter Seven

The Zim line ship *Sara* was being nudged gently and slowly toward the stone quay. The first officer reported from the communication post in the bow to the command deck: "First rope on shore."

"Easy to port," called the French navigator in heavily accented English that all but twisted the words beyond recognition.

The man at the wheel loudly repeated his own Hebrew version of the English command and held the half-moon-shaped wheel steady as the red needle indicated five degrees. The tug boat's propellers stirred up a heavy wake of foam as the side of the *Sara* gradually approached the quay.

Gad Ullman stood in total darkness near the window at the front of the visitors' compartment. As he put on his short jacket, moving slowly and methodically, his eye finally found what he had been looking for. There was a car with diplomatic plates waiting for him, parked only a few yards from the water's edge. From long experience he knew that it would be an embassy car driven by a Mossad man from the Foreign Relations Division.

Gad Ullman moved from the visitors' compartment only

when he saw through the window that the first officer had left the communication post. The two men met near the door of the special storeroom with its sealed locker that was fixed to the masthead between storage areas one and two. The ship's officer pulled a bunch of keys from his pocket. He opened the two heavy locks hanging on the door, then called over two sailors. They lifted the long, heavy, metal box and carefully carried it toward the gangway, keeping a wary eye on the strange passenger who had unexpectedly joined the ship just before sailing from Haifa. The box was heavily stamped with customs clearances and was marked *"Diplomatic Shipment,"* with the name of Ullman's country in large letters. It contained the tools of his trade as "Exterminator."

Gad Ullman walked ahead of the little group as though they did not exist. In his hand he carried a leather briefcase. The car with the diplomatic plates drew nearer, coming to a stop only when it seemed on the verge of toppling into the sea.

The sailors knew better than to chat, let alone joke with the skinny, fragile-looking man in front of them. Although he gave the impression of being so feeble that he might be unable to carry even the small case in his hand, they had learned in the course of the journey to give him a wide berth. They were convinced he was a nasty, disagreeable snob; he had ignored all their friendly overtures to join in conversation. Even when they ate together, he hardly replied when spoken to. No one had heard him exchange a single word with anyone. It was as though he were deaf and dumb. Once in a while, he had climbed from his cabin to the command deck to take some air, but even then he stood by himself and declined to mix with the officers.

Gad Ullman was not in the slightest disturbed by the fact that he was intensely disliked. The crew knew he was a fellow countryman; one of them had heard him greet the skipper in Hebrew on his arrival. It was, in fact, the only time any of them had heard him speak.

The "Exterminator" was not trying to be disagreeable. He was on a mission, and until he had achieved his objective he did not consider himself like other men. At the moment he cared nothing for affection or hate or any other emotion. As he explained it, there was no room for such luxuries when the red light of the killer had been switched on. He was no longer Gad Ullman, civil servant, husband of an adoring wife and father of three small children. He was a cold, calculating exterminator.

He remembered the time when he had been sent to a small village in Austria to track down a concentration camp doctor who was leading a new and peaceful life under an assumed name. The ex-Nazi had given shelter to three former death camp guards who lived at his home and worked officially as his "gardeners." In reality, they were there to protect him, even though the war had been over for many years and the doctor, who had carried out surgical experiments on children without any kind of anesthetic, was convinced that he had covered his tracks completely.

When Mike had spelled out some of the crimes the doctor had been guilty of, Gad had cut him short. "Just provide me with his photograph," he said. It was clear from his attitude that he was not really interested in the man's background. If he was ordered to wipe him out, that was what he would do. Once he had candidly told his commander: "It doesn't really matter about the man's record. When I am hunting him down, I never let my emotions enter into it. I have no moral reservations or *angst,* as they put it. It's a job. I do it. I am a professional. Just give me the details."

To avoid "diplomatic problems" it had been decided to put an end to the doctor without revealing his true identity to the authorities in Vienna. The Austrians had a record of dragging their feet in such cases, and many high officials in government service still had a sneaking sympathy for Hitler and his ideas.

The problem was the guards, who never let the doctor out of their sight. They were grateful for the refuge and steady employment with which he had provided them, and they protected him as though their own lives depended on it, as indeed they did.

For two entire days and nights Ullman lay in ambush at the top of the local church tower. He had jammed wads of cotton into his ears to drown out the chiming of the clock and the tolling of the bells. Then, from a distance of three hundred feet, he had shot the doctor through the temple. No one heard the shot. The ex-Nazi had stepped out of the kitchen door to get something from the adjacent garage while his "gardeners" sat indoors watching television. His crumpled body was found ten minutes later, surrounded by a neat pool of blood.

The closest that Ullman had ever come to disaster was when he was sent to Montevideo to kill one of the most infamous Nazis of all, Herbert Zukors, "the Hangman of Riga." Zukors was accused of killing some thirty thousand men, women, and children—most of them Jews—in his native city. He was not a German but had eagerly joined the Nazis when they came marching into his country. "The Hangman of Riga" had participated so enthusiastically in the killing of his victims that he won the praise of Adolf Eichmann, the Nazi leader in charge of the Jewish extermination program.

At the end of the war, Zukors had made his escape in the company of a Jewish girl whom he had saved from a concentration camp. In Brazil, where his true record was not known, he was welcomed as a hero by the local Jewish community in the city of São Paulo.

Unfortunately for him, Zukors could not hold his liquor; he spoke too freely in the crowded bars of São Paulo. He had, however, taken the precaution of being surrounded by bodyguards. Wherever he went, he was armed with a switchblade knife attached to his left wrist and a Luger revolver in a shoulder holster. These precautions were doubled after the Mossad kidnapped Adolf Eichmann from his hideout in Buenos Aires. Eventually Zukors was tricked by another "ex-S.S. army officer" on the run, a blond Aryan, who in reality was a Mossad agent operating under the code name of "Kitzla." He persuaded Zukors to come to the Uruguayan capital where Gad Ullman was waiting for him.

The "Exterminator" often thought of that evening. It was warm and humid; his shirt had stuck to his back, unlike the comfort of his air-conditioned office in Tel Aviv. On his lap was a Beretta .22; he often used this efficient weapon. True, it was a low-caliber pistol but a specially designed device perfected by Mossad experts gave it a surprisingly forceful blast. As he knew from past experience, a hit from a distance of a few yards was more deadly and even more devastating than one from a .45.

Zukors was just about to cross the threshold of the room when he froze. The instinct of the hunter warned him of danger. Gad Ullman had waited calmly, his face half-hidden in the semidarkness of the room. The eyes of the two men met for a fraction of a second.

The tall Nazi moved with amazing speed despite his sixty-five years. The Luger was in his hand in a flash. But Gad had raised his Beretta even faster. The .22 bullet crashed into Zukor's chest, sliced through the left ventricle, and finally lodged in one of his ribs, as the Uruguay police later verified when they found his body.

Even so, he had managed to get one shot in, lightly grazing Gad's arm, before the impact of the Beretta's bullet sent him spinning backward. Ullman was so upset about it that for months after his return to Tel Aviv he doubled the time spent on the practice range at Mossad headquarters.

Now as the "Exterminator" left the *Sara*, the man waiting for him near the green Ford Cortina approached the gangway in order to help the sailors who were struggling with the metal case. They deposited it by the luggage compartment of the car.

Opening the trunk with his key, the chauffeur signaled to the crewmen to place the case inside. Without a word, he motioned the thin passenger to climb into the vehicle. Seconds later the car was moving away—even before the ship was completely tied up to the quayside. Gad Ullman had not said farewell to either the sailors or their officers. He left as he had arrived, mysteriously and anonymously.

The two men passed through customs control without any difficulty. A junior official stamped their papers without asking to see the box. Another customs official wrote something illegible on it when the trunk was opened and then ordered the guard stationed near the barrier to let the car pass. The Cortina crossed the center of the city and then swung onto the highway leading to Paris.

Hardly a word passed between the two men. Two hours after setting off, Gad Ullman curtly requested the driver to pull off the main highway onto a side road. Spotting an isolated wood, he asked his companion to drive into it on a dirt track until they were well hidden from all passing traffic. The "Exterminator" got out of the car and looked carefully around him. When he was sure no other vehicle had followed them, he ordered the driver to unlock the trunk. Then tearing the lead seal off the box, he took two keys from his pocket and opened it.

The driver tried to peer over the shoulder of his thin passenger, but all he managed to see was a slender leather holster with a small-caliber Beretta pistol inside it; the holster strap had two magazines with bullets fixed diagonally.

Gad Ullman stripped off his jacket. Working swiftly and professionally, as though he had done it hundreds of times before, he placed the holster under his arm. The wooden tray on which the pistol had rested covered the interior of the box and completely hid its contents. Without a word of explanation, Gad locked the box with both keys. He walked over toward a clump of trees and meticulously checked the pistol, examined the bullet magazine, tried the cocking device, and then, apparently finally satisfied, returned the weapon to the holster. He then adjusted the holster with the same care and attention he had given the pistol.

It took several minutes before he was satisfied that it fitted comfortably. Then he drew the gun from the holster again and again and once more adjusted its position. Finally he placed the weapon back in the holster, put on his jacket, and carefully buttoned it. With a curt nod of his head he indicated to the driver that it was time to press on.

They drove for hours without exchanging a word. Twice he instructed the puzzled chauffeur to make a sudden detour, asking him not to indicate that he was going to turn off the main road in advance. Both times it was to verify that they were not being followed.

On those occasions when they had to pull up for fuel, they did so quickly. The driver had the tank filled; he was then told to go to a nearby restaurant and get sandwiches and cold drinks, but "to hurry up about it." There was no time even for calls of nature on these stops. When they had to relieve themselves, it was always done at the roadside, away from other cars, behind trees or in ditches. The passenger wanted to avoid meeting people at all costs; it was as if he had leprosy.

Only when they were nearing Antwerp, their destination, did Gad Ullman suggest that they change places for a while so the driver could get a well-earned rest. Even at the wheel of the car the mysterious passenger was as reticent and taciturn as he had been throughout the long journey. It was late at night when they reached the outskirts of the Belgian city.

Chapter Eight

It was impossible to mistake the gait of the broad-shoul-dered passenger in the gray suit who stepped out of the El Al plane that landed at Brussels airport. He was a man of the sea. And to judge by the look on his face he was glad to be back on the ground. In his hand he carried a croco-dile suitcase that was just large enough to slide under the airline seat. He had no other luggage.

The passport control officer glanced quickly at his British passport, checked to see if the photograph of "James Williams" matched the face of the passenger, and signaled him through.

"Anything to declare?" asked the customs man.

"No," replied the businessman. Again he was nodded through without any delay.

There was no one waiting for "James Williams" among the crowds that had come to meet incoming passengers. He climbed into the first available taxi and in passable French asked to be taken to the central railway station. Once there, he wasted no time. He immediately bought a first-class ticket for Antwerp.

The Belgian authorities were not then to know it, but

"James Williams" was not James Williams. Nor was he a British citizen. He was the Israeli skipper Ze'ev Biran.

Opposite the entrance of the old railway station in Antwerp a black Citroën was waiting for him. Ze'ev hurried across the street toward it and shook hands with the blond driver. The driver was in a hurry; the car was moving before Biran had even slammed the passenger door.

A mere thirty-six hours before this meeting, an orange-colored Scania trailer truck had driven up to the western gate of Rotterdam harbor. The two men seated inside it sat patiently facing the central customs warehouse, waiting their turn. In their hands were documents indicating that they worked for Arisal-Kopke, a German company. They were instructed to transport a cargo container which included electric generators and industrial electronic equipment for delivery to the company's Amsterdam branch. According to the registration papers, the machinery had been shipped to the port from Genoa on an Israeli vessel, the *Etrog*.

The customs officer examined their bills of lading. He checked the registration, then stenciled a small cross beside the space where the merchandise was described. Politely he directed the driver toward the large warehouse right at the other end of the dock. The orange-colored truck moved slowly between the trolleys crammed with crates which were being unloaded from the ships berthed alongside the docks.

The two men had no difficulty in spotting the sealed blue container that they had come for. The company's name was boldly stenciled in large white letters on all four sides. The warehouse foreman seemed happy enough to get rid of the large container, since the building was filled to capacity with goods waiting for clearance. The container the men had come for was standing awkwardly right in the center of the warehouse, obstructing the movement of the fork-lift vehicles.

The foreman did not stop to examine the list of contents of the offending container. He hastily signed the release form and told them in a grumbling voice: "We're swamped with work right now. I'm short-staffed, there's some kind of 'flu epidemic . . ." He signaled to a fork-truck operator standing near the warehouse gate to handle the job.

The man maneuvered his hoisting vehicle skillfully, and the heavy blue container rose in the air as though it were a feather being blown gently upward by a puff of wind. Confidently he headed toward the truck whose wooden panels had been removed. Treating the container as though it held fragile china, he lowered it gently onto the platform of the Scania and smiled at the two men. It was the smile of a skilled craftsman who took pride in his work.

The truck driver signed the forms thrust in front of him by the foreman. Payment of the port charges and receipt of the final authorization in the customs office near the gate took no longer than a few minutes. The two men secured the steel cables, which were passed along the length of the container and fastened on the other side of the truck with a tightening screw. They tested it thoroughly. Confident at last that it was secure, they climbed into the cab of their truck and drove off.

Chapter Nine

Sharon's relationship with the Italian official of Euratom flowered rapidly. There was a mutual physical attraction. Antonio Bordini was fascinated by the aura of mystery that surrounded this American woman, who he became convinced very quickly was more than a mere fashion photographer. He was aware that she was feeding his pro-Israeli sympathies with odd remarks and comments, but he had no objection.

Sharon played her hand carefully. One morning she hinted that she would "like to do more for Israel than simply offer verbal support." Carefully the Euratom executive answered that he shared her sentiments entirely. A little later Sharon revealed that she had a very good friend, Paul, who happened to be connected with Israeli intelligence. She hastily added that she did not know exactly what he did, but thought how nice it would be if she had a party and the two men could meet.

"But I don't want you to tell him that I suspect he is involved with some kind of intelligence work," she made Antonio promise. "I am just guessing really."

The Italian took to her friend immediately, particularly when he discovered that Paul was the brother of her pilot friend who had died in the Six-Day War. Since Paul was "happily married with two small children," there was no question of his being a rival for Sharon's affections. Paul's wife was in Tel Aviv awaiting the birth of her third child.

On several occasions the trio was seen together in Brussels restaurants and cafés. Antonio was delighted to have Paul's company. In fact, he was more than willing to fall in with any of Sharon's suggestions—she had made a very deep impression on him. Paul, who always insisted on paying, was a most generous host. Once when Antonio tried to pick up the bill, Sharon whispered to him, after their companion had left them to make a telephone call: "You know I am *sure* he is in the intelligence. I have a suspicion that he's the guy who has his hands on the purse-strings. He is ready to pay a lot of money, thousands of dollars, for information at times. Although I haven't the faintest idea what information he likes to collect."

Antonio Bordini now seized the bait that had been enticingly dangled before his nose. Whether or not he saw through Sharon's maneuvers was something he kept to himself. On the day after the talk of "thousands of dollars," he telephoned Paul and suggested that the Israeli meet him at a café in Brooker Square. He did not want Sharon to be there.

The Italian came straight to the point. "I know you are involved in some kind of espionage work," he said.

Paul looked shocked and surprised and was about to make a firm denial when Antonio interrupted: "Listen. Don't kid me. Your secret is absolutely safe with me. I am sure Sharon has told you that your people have my total sympathy. I have been thinking the matter over and I would like to help you. And of course I am sure that you in turn will help me a little."

Paul continued to look perplexed. "I don't know what you . . ."

"Listen," said Bordini, irritated now. He wondered if he was not making a fool of himself, if Sharon had not made a dreadful mistake. After all, it is a very romantic notion to tell your friends that you know a real live James Bond spy. He pressed the point: "I have information I *know* will be of considerable use to you."

Paul leaned forward, his voice a mere whisper: "What sort of information?"

Bordini explained briefly the sort of work he did at Euratom. Judging by the expression on the face of the Israeli, his words were not making much impression. So he came right out with it: "I have information regarding the transfer of uranium within Europe and to Common Market countries."

Bordini swallowed hard. He found it difficult to say the next words, for he knew that with them he was betraying the trust placed in him. However, the die was cast.

"I know that France in the past has transferred uranium to your people at Dimona out of its own quota of stocks. We even have a special code for these shipments. I also know that the shipments have ceased."

He leaned back in his seat. Suddenly his mouth was very dry. He took a sip from the Campari he was drinking and added: "As a matter of fact, you weren't the only customers of the French. Nor are the French the only ones involved in passing on uranium to particular friends. Now, what I have is information that——"

Paul cut him short. "It all sounds very interesting. But it's not really my line. Can you give me twenty-four hours? I'll come up with an answer."

Bordini suddenly realized he was engaged in a kind of game and that he was being asked to observe the rules.

"Take as long as you want," he said with a smile. Paul smiled back with his face and lips; Antonio Bordini noticed that his eyes had no laughter in them. They were hard and suddenly very frightening. The Italian shivered even though it was a hot summer's day and he was warmly dressed.

The two men met again thirty-six hours later. Paul had arranged that they meet in Bordini's apartment. The Israeli agent placed a fat brown envelope on the table. In it were twenty crisp new five-hundred-dollar bills.

"This is an advance," Paul said. "I know some people who are willing to pay much more for up-to-date information on the movement of cargoes of uranium and their timetables."

That evening, seeing a cigar butt in an ashtray in Antonio's living room, Sharon guessed that "Paul" had been there. She looked at Bordini with innocent surprise on her face. "Isn't it dangerous for you to meet a man who is an Israeli agent?"

Bordini was embarrassed. He blustered and raised his voice, then finally admitted rather tamely that Paul *had* called.

Sharon was upset. "I am not trying to pry into your affairs," she said, being contrite. "But you know as well as I do that Brussels is full of spies and espionage agents."

It was true. Ever since the Belgian city had become the virtual capital of the Common Market and various EEC organizations had moved their headquarters there, it had become a major magnet for intelligence agencies from all over the world.

"If you are seen mixing with such people you know that your job will be immediately at stake. I just don't want you to get into trouble, that's all—after all, I introduced you to Paul. My conscience would never rest if I was indirectly responsible for causing you harm!"

Bordini was deeply touched. He could hardly hide from Sharon the fact that he *was* meeting Paul. So a delicate "arrangement" was made. Sharon was to act as the "contact" between Antonio Bordini and Paul. Sharon simply handed envelopes from her friend to the Italian, and he in turn would give her large packets of documents. That way no one would be endangered. From that moment on, the three were never seen together again.

Less than a week after this happy system was under way, Sharon was standing by the window on the fifth floor of the Palace Hotel, looking down into the street below. Behind her, the man sitting at the desk suddenly let out a whistle. She turned to "Paul"—better known to her as Mike. He was examining a sheaf of papers and photostat copies of documents that were stamped with a variety of classifications ranging from "Highly Confidential" to "Secret." One had caught his attention.

Mike got up suddenly and went over to the telephone on the small table next to the bed. After dialing a number, he closely studied the document that had come from Antonio Bordini, then said to whoever answered the phone, "Find out why the Moroccans are trying to get their hands on the stuff. What use do they have for the kind of material we're after? Also try to find out if they have machines like ours. And what tricks they use to get hold of the goods they need."

The voice at the other end was so clear Sharon could hear the answer: "I'll have to look into the first matter. The second I can tell you right away—no, they don't have machines like ours. But they've been considered associate members of the Common Market for some time. This status allows them to acquire the uranium after it's been given a certain treatment that insures it can be used for industrial purposes only. It's no good as war material in this form. In any event, the Moroccans don't even have sufficiently advanced technology to use uranium for ordinary industrial purposes."

Both men were obviously puzzled by the information that Mike had found so fascinating.

"Find out everything you can about Moroccan industrial development," he said casually. Sharon could sense that a red light was flashing in his head.

With the instincts of a born intelligence man, Mike knew that he was on to something.

"I want the information by tomorrow."

Chapter Ten

Colonel Habib Boudija was a young and idealistic lieutenant when he was first assigned to the Moroccan secret service. This was in the days when the French were still in control of that North African country. He had been educated by French teachers, and he owed his army training to the French, but like so many of his countrymen he hated the "colonial oppressors." He was well paid by the French security services who had also trained him. However, this did not stop him from joining the Moroccan resistance movement. Thus he came to know the leaders of the underground.

Later, he was to turn this information to good account. A large number of these nationalists were also hostile to the monarch, King Mohammed V, who took over the running of the country when the French departed; many of them started plotting against the king. Because Colonel Habib Boudija knew exactly who he was looking for and where they liked to hide in the teeming casbahs of the country's larger cities, he gained a remarkable record for tracking down his former friends.

In 1956, when Morocco achieved its independence, Boudija was asked to join the group whose job it was to set up the country's security service. Luckily for him, he was a personal friend of the chief of the newly created *Deuxième Bureau*, General Muhammed Ofkir. Sensing that Ofkir was going to be a great power in the land, Colonel Habib served him faithfully and well. Rapid promotion followed this shrewd move. A mere eight years after the wild celebrations in Morocco that marked the departure of the "oppressors" from the shores of his country, Colonel Boudija was appointed head of the Moroccan secret service for all of Europe.

This was his real role although officially his name appeared as Assistant Attaché for Cultural Affairs in the Moroccan embassy in Paris. This cover enabled him to move quite freely among the Common Market countries and provided the ideal opportunity for his numerous missions to every part of Europe.

The colonel was an impressive and handsome man. He wore a thin, neatly trimmed moustache that superbly underlined his deep-set black eyes. He fancied himself a potential movie star, and his friends knew that the best way to flatter him when favors were needed was to comment on how much he looked like that great Hollywood legend, Errol Flynn.

Habib Boudija behaved with flamboyant and exaggerated chivalry toward women. With men he liked to maintain an image of toughness and ruthlessness by deliberately exaggerating the various cruelties he had used on those enemies unfortunate enough to fall into his hands. It pleased him immeasurably to know that among the staff his nickname was the "Shark."

He looked amiable enough now as he sat in his armchair in the security officers' room at the Moroccan embassy in the French capital, skimming through agents' reports and making notes on a pad at his side. He was just about to start reading the contents of a pile of registered letters that had reached him from Rabat when he noticed a memo wedged among the correspondence.

Suddenly he sat bolt upright. With a sense of urgency he pressed the button of the intercom on the desk and roared into it: "Khalid, when did the call from Roget arrive?"

A young man with prominent cheekbones and a

frightened look on his face came running into the room. He could tell from the tone of the boss's voice that he was extremely angry. He looked at the memo in his own handwriting on the paper with the embassy letterhead. *Roget telephoned.* A telephone number was recorded neatly beside the man's name.

"Ten minutes before you arrived, *mon colonel,*" he replied.

"Don't just stand there like a donkey. Get him right away!"

Roget was the code name Mike used in their contacts with each other. Boudija knew Mike well—only too well. If he had telephoned and left his number, it was not to inquire about the colonel's health. It meant business—urgent business.

The voice at the other end showed no particular emotion. Colonel Boudija recognized it right away. It was the man who had an awesome reputation as head of the Mossad's Special Operations Division.

To an outsider it might have seemed strange that there was a link between an Israeli secret service man and a Moroccan. Officially at least, the two countries were hostile to one another. But the world of espionage is never straightforward. Secret service agents frequently cooperate with seemingly bitter enemies if it is in the mutual interest of both parties. It is never done officially and any mention of such "mutual help" will always be promptly denied by government spokesmen if such matters reach the newspapers.

In the early 1960s both Morocco and Israel saw in Egypt's President Gamal Abdul Nasser a mutually dangerous foe. There was, in the delicate explanation offered by a man involved at the time in the link between the two countries, "an understanding." It was an understanding that was in turn linked with further mutual cooperation with other western intelligence services. As an example of this "cooperation," French security forces were given a tip from Mossad agents that President Charles de Gaulle was going to be assassinated on a particular day at a particular spot by certain ex-settlers from Algeria. The French were grateful, and in the fall of 1965 when Ahmed Ben Barka, the left-wing Moroccan, came to Paris, they did Israeli intelligence a favor that resulted in an international incident and caused grave embarrassment to the official French government.

As a result of this favor, General Ofkir was able to save his king from losing his crown. Consequently, Ofkir owed some people favors, and high on that list was Mike of the Mossad.

Now the same Mike was speaking to the general's man, Colonel Boudija. "Hello, Habib. Can we talk?"

The colonel signaled to Khalid to clear out of his office. There was no mistaking the gesture. Even so, the Moroccan security man was cautious: "If it is business, it would be better to meet somewhere . . ."

"Café Sélect?"

"*D'accord*." Okay. The two men always spoke French to one another, even though the Mossad commander could speak perfect Arabic.

Mike was troubled. He knew Boudija well. At one stage he had even agreed to help train some of the Moroccan agents in modern methods of espionage; the colonel had been one of his pupils. It would have amazed most people to learn that a group of Moroccans had traveled secretly to Israel where they were given a course of instruction. Mike himself had conducted the classes. There was, however, an ulterior motive in this apparent act of generosity. He wanted to know everything about these men whom he would, in all probability, one day count among his foes.

Boudija had been the pick of the bunch. The Mossad had studied him closely, but had concluded that he was "not good material." He was arrogant and lazy. He was also totally corrupt. But he did have one sterling quality—he was extremely cunning and could think with the speed of a striking snake. Mike had no illusions. Boudija was dangerous, very dangerous, and not to be trusted under any circumstances.

However, in the matter at hand, the Mossad commander had no choice. The only way to reach General Muhammed Ofkir was through the colonel. So be it, he thought to himself, as he sat waiting at the Sélect for Boudija.

He liked the café, for patrons could be totally inconspicuous no matter what their business. It was filled with students and other young people determined to show society and the world at large that they were "different." Some wore long hair and outlandish clothes. Homosexuals and lesbians openly flaunted their unconventional behavior as if deliberately taunting any bourgeois elements who happened to be present. Not far from where Mike was sitting two long-haired men were kissing each other. One tall and very thin youth with a single gold earring tried without success to interest Mike in a pamphlet on how to join a secret Satanic society that carried out its mysterious and exciting rites in a nearby house.

Two tables away sat a very sad-looking girl with a head of curly hair and extremely sensuous lips. Mike smiled at her automatically. She got up and approached his table with a sad smile of her own. She was very pretty and the Mossad commander instantly realized that she was also very hungry. He looked up at a passing waitress and ordered her to bring the girl some steak and french fries. The girl stared hard at Mike, then said: "I am Juliette. You can sleep with me if you wish."

"Maybe another time," he responded, and then told her to return to her own table where her dinner would soon be served. From the corner of his eye he had spotted Boudija crossing the street and approaching the café. Through the wide window he also noticed the broad-shouldered "gorilla" walking at Boudija's side.

With professional interest the Mossad commander watched the colonel order his bodyguard to enter the café first. The "gorilla" did so. His eyes skimmed over the patrons and then came to rest on Mike. He had taken in and made note of a rather kinky-looking man in torn and jagged jeans sitting near the bar whose disinterest in what was happening at the neighboring tables was a bit too elaborate. So the Mossad man had *his* "gorilla" too.

Mike smiled. The colonel had not altogether wasted his time during the training period. In any event, it is difficult for an agent to mislead a professional colleague who had been well instructed in surveillance techniques. Today the rules of the game were being scrupulously followed; both men were protected by skilled marksmen.

The colonel walked straight to Mike's table after a quick nod from his "gorilla." Just as he was about to speak, the girl with the sad eyes walked up to Mike, bent over and kissed him squarely on the lips. Calmly she returned to her table to devour the meal that had been placed in front of her.

"I see they still fall in love with you at first sight," said the Moroccan, extremely impressed. "I have always admired this quality of yours."

Mike drew a piece of paper from his pocket. It was a photograph of a legal document although the lettered heading had been cut off to avoid identification.

"I have asked you to meet me because you owe us a debt. It is a debt of honor between myself and the general."

The colonel smiled broadly and fingered his moustache. "Funny thing," he said. "Somehow I knew when I got your message that that would be the topic of conversation. How do you want us to repay you?"

Mike glanced at the document in front of him. "According to my information two hundred tons of uranium oxide, known in the trade as 'yellowcake,' are being delivered to you in Antwerp in two months' time. It is going to sail on November 17th. It has been bought on behalf of Chimagar, a Casablanca chemical company."

Mike pressed home his attack. "Chimagar isn't interested in uranium. They don't even know they've bought the stuff. The company that purchased the uranium in their name is a German firm called Asmara. It was set up by a man named Herbert Scharf. And we've discovered that the buyer for Asmara is a Herr Herbert Schulzen. These are the gentlemen responsible for getting the yellowcake and sending it to Casablanca. None of this is news to you. Now I know it too."

Without altering his low, even tone, Mike added: "We need that cargo."

The colonel whistled admiringly. The deal had presumably been made under conditions of air-tight top-priority secrecy. "Is that all you want?" he asked. "Are you telling me that you want a whole ship to disappear?"

"Not disappear," Mike replied. "We'll buy the ship from you, cargo included. The name of the company that will take over the vessel, on my behalf, is called the Biscayne Traders Shipping Corporation."

The colonel played for time desperately as he tried to figure out just how much Mike knew about the operation. "You realize, of course, that all this is beyond my control. I will have to refer the matter to the highest authorities. It's a question of national——"

Mike cut him short. "You know what I'm talking about. You don't have nuclear reactors. You don't need uranium. But you do happen to have better connections with a certain Eastern customer who does not have *your* excellent relations with Euratom. . . . I could go into more details which might cost some very high-level officials their jobs there. But I wouldn't want to embarrass you. That's not my concern anyway. I want that cargo."

Colonel Habib Boudija looked right back into Mike's eyes. "I know you Israelis *do* have a reactor. I have also done my homework. I also know that in the right hands that uranium can be converted into something like thirty nuclear bombs."

Mike was not to be drawn into such speculations. "There's no room for blackmail," he said crisply. "The French have cut off our supplies of uranium. That you know. We need the uranium for research purposes. Without uranium we cannot continue our research."

Boudija reacted just as Mike knew he would. He wanted a bribe.

"How much in money is it worth to you?"

"The market price for the uranium is roughly three and a half million dollars," said Mike. "Let's say we can arrange a ten percent commission and something for possible damages and expenses. The money will be paid in cash in . . . wherever you want it paid."

The waitress set two cups of coffee on the table. Neither man touched his. They were watching each other closely.

"It's a delicate matter. I'll have to check," said the Moroccan.

Mike drew an oblong unmarked brown envelope from his pocket. "Here's a return ticket to Rabat plus five thousand dollars for your expenses and any inconvenience you've been caused. I need the general's answer in twenty-four hours. Otherwise the deal is off."

The colonel looked pained. He tried to protest and made a weak effort to return the envelope. He knew and

Mike knew that he could fly back free any time—first class—to his homeland. The five thousand dollars and the money from the ticket would go straight into his own pocket.

Both men rose. "I'll get you a reply in twenty-four hours," said the Moroccan as he hastily thrust the envelope into his inside breast pocket.

"Please do that," said Mike. "Give the general my best wishes and tell him that his consent will settle the account between us."

Mike stayed behind to pay the waitress for the steak and the coffee. The girl with the sad eyes was now sitting next to a very young man who was holding both her hands in his. His long hair reached below his shoulders. The girl did not even notice as Mike got up to go.

He sighed in regret and left the café. The man sitting near the bar slid off his stool and followed his boss at a discreet distance.

It was 10:20 A.M. Air France flight 937 to Rabat had arrived eight minutes late. Colonel Habib Boudija was among the last to leave the aircraft. A large man with narrow eyes and a prominent forehead met him near the runway and silently took the black attaché case—his only luggage. A second man, also powerfully built, opened the back door of the black Cadillac waiting on the tarmac and the colonel climbed in. The car headed for the general's offices which were located on the other side of the city. As head of the security services as well as commander of the army and minister of the interior, General Ofkir occupied a luxurious suite in the largest office building in the city, a sixteen-story structure. From there, the most powerful man in the country conducted his various official duties.

The car traveled at an infuriatingly slow speed. Repair work on the main road from the airport to the city had been going on for years, and the highway seemed to be even more chaotic than ever. At the entrance to Rabat the Cadillac was caught up in a vast traffic jam caused by a collision between a taxi and a horse-drawn cart. The animal lay dead in the middle of the road, surrounded by crates of oranges spilled in every direction. The driver went to investigate and returned roaring with laughter.

"There is also a truck wrapped around the traffic light," he reported.

The colonel was furious. "Why is it that it always happens here? Things like this never happen in Europe."

The colonel's companions stopped laughing. They knew that although Habib Boudija, like many men who had served under the French, pretended to hate the colonizers, he now behaved as though he was a French administrator, finding fault with everything in the country. In his homeland, the colonel frequently started conversations with the phrase: "In Europe this wouldn't happen . . ."

Boudija still eulogized the French and, like General Ofkir, was often heard to say: "I give you my word of honor as a former French officer." For a man who had fought to expel the "oppressors," he never stopped to think how strange his comments were.

The colonel and his two companions walked for a while, then finally hailed a taxi which made its way slowly past caravans of camels and mules, down narrow streets filled with stalls that jutted out at all angles. Men and women wandered at will all over the road, oblivious of the cars.

Once at Ofkir's office the colonel was kept waiting for a while in the visitors' room; a meeting of the military affairs committee was in progress. However, Ofkir's secretary promised Boudija that he would not have long to wait. That, as he knew full well, could mean anything from ten minutes to several hours.

The colonel was uneasy. General Ofkir was the only man whom he truly feared. As he waited, he clenched and unclenched his fists nervously and gazed up at the portrait of the king, a smiling, handsome man. "He can afford to smile—as long as he is assured of the general's loyalty," he said—but quietly, to himself.

At the age of forty-four, General Muhammed Ofkir was the real ruler of Morocco. He could arrest or execute almost anyone in the country without trial, without even bothering to mention the matter to the king. For his part, the monarch knew that he could trust the general completely. As long as he had Ofkir's support his throne was absolutely safe from his vast array of enemies, internal and external.

His most formidable foe had been the socialist leader Ben Barka. Under his dynamic leadership all the opposition groups of the left had buried their differences, uniting to overthrow the monarch and convert the country into a "people's democracy." Muhammed Ofkir, on the other hand, was no revolutionary. He had already saved the king from several assassination attempts. The only thing that interested him was power—total power.

The son of a rich Berber landholder from the Atlas Mountains, Ofkir despised the Arabs who had subjugated his non-Muslim fellow tribesmen. He had been educated by the French colonial administration and had served them faithfully. To this day he admired the order and discipline the French had introduced to Morocco. With all his heart he had wanted to be accepted by the French as one of their own. To this end he enrolled in a French army officers school.

A brave man who never feared death, he had volunteered for a French commando unit during the Second World War, and was frequently cited in dispatches and given medals for his bravery in battle. He had been seriously wounded by a German flame-thrower, and the ugly scars that covered his face were for him a source of pride.

Then his regiment was transferred to Indochina. It was here that Ofkir learned a new art—that of torture. Like everything else he involved himself in, he studied the subject thoroughly. So impressed were his superiors with his newly acquired skills that he was appointed chief interrogation officer. His instructors, however, were not Frenchmen. In fact, many in the army disapproved of using torture, and so Muhammed Ofkir sought inspiration from the Viet Cong, who knew no rivals in this art of persuasion and "political education."

On one occasion the young Moroccan was instructed to take a patrol on a six-day mission through enemy-controlled rice paddies and villages. There were two purposes to the exercise: to demonstrate that they had the talent to survive under such conditions and also to try and make contact with a similar group reported missing in the same area four days earlier. The lieutenant led his fifteen men as they followed the tracks of the lost patrol.

When they finally found them, some of the most

toughened soldiers had to avert their eyes, and others turned their backs and quietly vomited at the roadside, hoping their companions would not notice.

Ofkir had no such inhibitions. He walked up boldly to the bodies skewered on sharpened bamboo canes in the middle of the abandoned village. There was no one around to tell the Moroccan what had happened, but all the evidence he needed was right there before his eyes. He examined the bodies of the tortured Frenchmen closely. Some had had their eyes slowly pried out of their heads with knives while still alive. Some had had pieces of wood driven through each finger. Others had had their nostrils slit open. Still others had had their testicles cut open with knives or pieces of sharp bamboo. Most had had their knuckles broken, and pieces of wood had been lodged in different apertures of their bodies. The mutilated corpses were already stinking.

Later, when the colonel got his hands on some Viet Cong, or those he suspected of being sympathizers, he repeated the methods that he had witnessed while on this patrol. It took some experimenting before he managed to turn the crude beginnings into an exact art. The aim was to prolong the agony and not kill off the prisoner too quickly. Soon the young Moroccan was spoken of with awe throughout the entire French army. His proud boast was that he could make anyone—no matter how stubborn—admit anything. He invented some subtleties of his own that not even the Viet Cong had thought of.

Ofkir won more decorations in Indochina to add to the honors he had gained in Europe. When he returned to Morocco, he was appointed special adviser to the French commissioner there. When French rule reverted to the Moroccans and Mohammed V was no longer a puppet king in his country, Ofkir gathered around him a private army trained by himself in the arts of kidnapping, murder, and torture. This was the cadre on which he built the country's *Deuxième Bureau.*

The old king was quick to see the value of a man like Ofkir. He made him a general and gave him immense power. His son King Hassan quickly got the message too. If anything, under his rule the general became even more powerful.

Ofkir had a genius for intelligence work. Soon his spies and his espionage network had spread throughout North Africa; its tentacles reached into every major European capital. By the end of 1963, the general's name was high on President Nasser's list of "men to be exterminated." This animosity arose after the Egyptian dictator was rash enough to send tank reinforcements to the Algerian army during border skirmishes between that country and its neighbor, Morocco. The price for this gesture of "brotherhood" to the Algerians was the lives of five senior Egyptian officers who had the misfortune to make a forced helicopter landing on Moroccan territory. There were no bamboo shoots around, but even so, the tortures inflicted on the Egyptians before they were handed back alive—but broken for life in body and spirit, and castrated for good measure—made a striking impression on President Nasser. He swore vengeance and sent secret agents to assassinate both Ofkir and his master, the Moroccan king. None of the agents was ever heard of again.

It was at this stage that Ahmed Ben Barka arrived on the scene. Sponsored by Cairo and Moscow, this revolutionary gathered around him all the opposition to the king's reign in Morocco. It was the gravest menace ever faced by General Ofkir, and he sent some of his best men to kill Ben Barka. Their remains were returned to him not long afterward in two sealed packages. The general tried again—using a letter bomb. This failed too, as did another attempt to assassinate Ben Barka in Geneva.

In the fall of 1965, President de Gaulle invited Ben Barka to visit Paris. This aroused the anger of Morocco's rulers, but the old general in the Elysée Palace could see that it was only a matter of time before Ben Barka would take over in his North African homeland. It was an astute move on the part of de Gaulle. In a single throw of the dice, he had stolen the game from Moscow. By recognizing the firebrand Moroccan leader he was hoping to ensure that, once in power, Ben Barka would shift from his extremist left-wing position and remain on good terms with France, rather than plunge his country into the communist camp.

By this time Ben Barka was considered more than just a revolutionary. He was taking on the mantle of a glamorous and charismatic figure, adored by liberals and the left wing of several countries as a sort of North African Che Guevara. However, Ben Barka had a particular hatred of Israelis, whom he considered an obstacle to his dreams of an emerging new power in the world—a united pan-Islam of all Arab states. Again and again he said: "Israel is a nuisance to be got rid of in order not to disturb the course of history." Thus Ben Barka had as many enemies as admirers in the chic left-bank salons of Paris and among the revolutionary-minded university students.

On his arrival in Paris, Ben Barka was given a warm welcome by the French government. It was arranged that he should meet the head of the cabinet, Georges Pompidou, before being ushered into the presence of de Gaulle himself. He was treated to the full panoply of French official splendor—with red carpets and much flag-waving.

The guard of honor that rode out to his hotel to escort the up-and-coming man of destiny reported that they had all left just as planned, dead on time. When last seen, Ben Barka was surrounded by four motorcyclists from the French security service, and three of his most trusted bodyguards were seated in the same official French government vehicle.

De Gaulle and Pompidou waited in vain for Ben Barka.

Neither he nor his bodyguards were ever seen alive again.

The scandal rocked France. Security chiefs were blasted by their president, who knew as well as anyone else how much Ben Barka was hated by most of the senior security officers. Shortly after Ben Barka's disappearance, a number of men, known to be members of various foreign intelligence services, who had made their base in Paris, suddenly went "on leave."

De Gaulle demanded that General Ofkir stand trial. Clearly his was the mastermind behind the disappearance of France's honored guest. But the Moroccan king stood firm. General Ofkir's head was not going to be handed on a plate to President de Gaulle. If anything, Ofkir's power increased. He had proved to his monarch that he was not only indispensable but the sure guarantor of the king's throne.

Muhammed Ofkir's office door opened and out stepped two army officers, one a general, the other a brigadier. Both greeted Colonel Boudija cordially, exchanged a few words of welcome, and then the visitor was shown into the room of his superior.

Ofkir greeted Boudija with a wide smile. His eyes, as usual, were covered by very dark glasses which only partially hid the damage done by one of Rommel's flamethrowers more than twenty years before. The glasses gave him an even more mysterious and sinister look than his reputation warranted. Because neither enemies nor friends could ever see what his eyes were really showing, the already formidable general had an even greater edge in dealing with visitors to his office.

Ofkir squeezed Boudija's outstretched hand without rising from his elegant leather armchair. He was not a man to waste time in idle talk. Before the colonel could ease himself into the proffered seat, the general asked bluntly: "What does our mutual friend want?"

The colonel had dreaded this moment. He knew that obliquely he would be blamed for the apparent leak of information that had obviously occurred in Europe. Girding himself, he plunged in.

"He wants the uranium shipment."

The general's face hardened into a stony mask. Muhammed was at his most venomous when his jaw tightened, as it now did. Habib Boudija could feel his spine tingle with fear.

"They know about the shipment?"

Boudija nodded. He did not trust his voice. The general was waiting for an explanation. Clearing his throat, the colonel tried to give it.

"I believe there has been a leak from Euratom. But I don't really think they know why the uranium is coming here."

Habib Boudija realized from the look on his chief's face that the man was not convinced. If the Mossad knew about the atomic reactor fuel that had been headed for Casablanca, then they must have discovered what its ultimate destination was.

"You can tell our friend to liberate uranium for somebody else. We cannot give the Israelis, of all people, preference over the Indians in this matter. We have an agreement to honor with them. We cannot violate it."

Colonel Habib Boudija did not relish having to spell all this out to Mike. The thought of the way his bank account was going to profit from a deal with the Mossad gave him the courage to speak out boldly: "Mike asked me to remind you that a debt of honor exists between yourself and him. He will consider it wiped out if he can get his hands on the cargo."

The word "honor" hit home.

"Why did he have to come to us at a time like this, dammit?" Ofkir did not really expect an answer.

Boudija continued: "They are really desperate. The French embargo has caught them with their pants down. I have checked out all the facts. Without our cargo of uranium they are paralyzed."

"So are the Indians," retorted the general. "Ever since Mrs. Gandhi revealed her own atomic weapons ambitions their sources of uranium have been cut off. We are their last hope. That's why they paid so much. Well, they have fulfilled their part of the bargain just as they promised they would—and what is more, they paid in gold. Still, we had a lot of problems to overcome too in order to get the uranium out of Euratom once they refused to let the shipment come direct to Casablanca as we had planned. The deal to send the uranium to that company in Genoa instead cost us twelve thousand dollars. What is their name again?" He searched for a document in his desk. "Ah, yes. *Società Anonima Italiana Colori e Affini.* SAICA for short." Both men laughed; by coincidence there was a Palestinian terrorist organization with similar initials.

The operation whereby the Moroccans were to provide Mrs. Gandhi with uranium had been skillfully thought out. As a first step in their master plan the Moroccans set up a company called Asmara Chemie in Wiesbaden, Germany. The company, under the control of Herbert Schulzen and Herbert Scharf, made a mistake at first and boldly set out to buy uranium openly on behalf of Chimagar, a seaweed processing company in Casablanca, although Chimagar had never before handled anything as complex as uranium. The contract for purchase from the Belgian company Société Générale des Minerais was signed on the 29th of March, 1968, almost eight months before the scheduled shipment to Antwerp. However, the Belgian authorities pointed out to Asmara that Euratom would never allow them to send uranium to Morocco as they planned. According to Euratom regulations, no nuclear material can be shipped to any country beyond the borders of the European community. And Morocco lay outside the Common Market.

But a loophole was found. Under Article 75 of the treaty which governs Euratom, uranium *can* be switched from one country to another *within* the Common Market. This is because it is not unusual for uranium to be sent to specialized factories for enrichment or other refining processes. The processed material must then be returned to the company that farmed it out.

So Asmara changed tack. It made a deal with SAICA, an Italian paint company, to process the material for them, although the firm had never before blended uranium. If the Milan company was surprised about the proposition they did not show it. Asmara explained that the process would be quite simple. The "other product" they wanted mixed with the uranium would be sent along as part of the same cargo, and instructions on what to do would be provided.

Twelve thousand dollars was handed over to the Italians as an advance payment. For security reasons, SAICA's chairman, Francesco Sertorio, was told that the 560 drums of yellowcake would be marked "plumbat," a name for a lead derivative. When the processing was complete, the "plumbat" was to be returned to Asmara in the same drums in which it had been delivered. Further details would be provided later.

Satisfied with the SAICA deal, Euratom supplied Asmara with the license to send the uranium by ship from Antwerp to Genoa. Instead of heading for the Italian port, however, the original Moroccan plan was to divert the ship to Casablanca, transfer the uranium to another vessel, and then send it on to India.

So now the general was worried. Any shift in plans meant trouble with India. And there would be trouble with Euratom too.

"Listen," Boudija said quietly and persuasively. "The

Indians can hardly voice any complaint. They can't tell the world that they were going to buy uranium illegally. And we can just deny it anyway. For that matter, you can give them back their gold if you want."

The thought almost made his stomach turn.

"It's to Israel's interest that no one knows anything. They'll keep it secret. And so will the Italians. We'll tell SAICA that we have made other arrangements and that they can keep the twelve thousand dollars for their inconvenience. Asmara Chemie can contact them later and explain.

"The uranium ship has to vanish anyway. Euratom will make inquiries eventually. But they'll do it quietly. They won't want to seem stupid, and in any case, there are ways of keeping them quiet."

At the thought of the bribe that was about to fall into his lap, Boudija waxed eloquent.

"And even if it does become public knowledge that the uranium ends up at Dimona, how can anyone point a finger at us? Are we not the sworn enemies of Zionism? Why we even sent some of our troops to help our Syrian brothers."

A flicker of a smile crossed the general's face. A Moroccan contingent *had* been sent by sea to Syria to fight the Zionists. By a strange coincidence all the officers dispatched to Syria were suspected of left-wing tendencies and some had even been plotting against the king. Consequently, the news that they had been badly battered by Israeli aircraft and had suffered severe casualties had not caused many tears in Ofkir's office.

Since General Ofkir continued to regard the colonel impassively, Boudija played his trump card. "I am ready to tell that son-of-a-whore Mike to go to hell if you wish. He can do nothing to us. He can get his uranium elsewhere. It hurts my ears, however, to hear him say it is question of honor. Your honor . . . But what do you care what he says?"

The barb sank in. The general moved to his desk. He lifted a gold paperweight and studied it pensively for a few seconds, then turned and spoke firmly to the colonel. His mind was made up.

"Tell him that the shipment is his. I will put no obstacles in his path. But I don't want to know anything more about the affair. You are now responsible for the whole business. You go over the essential details with him. Give him all the assistance he needs. I don't want any complaints from him."

General Ofkir looked hard at the colonel. A shiver of fear edged its way down Boudija's spine. It was now his baby. If anything went wrong, his head would be on the block. Above all, he had to be sure that the general's "honor" would in no way be impaired in the eyes of the Israeli.

Ofkir began thumbing through the papers on his desk. Boudija knew it was his signal to leave. As he rose and turned toward the door, the general said softly, in a voice filled with menace: "Tell that man whom I respect as a courageous agent—and whom you chose to call a son-of-a-whore—that I send him my best wishes."

At 11:15 P.M. the last Air France plane from Rabat landed at Orly Airport. Colonel Boudija was again among the last to disembark, but this time there was no car waiting for him on the tarmac. After all, in France he was no more than a mere assistant cultural attaché.

Once through passport and customs control he made straight for a telephone booth. Although the airport terminal was almost deserted, he made sure no one was standing at the neighboring booths before he dialed. The voice at the other end sounded sleepy.

"Ali speaking. I have something to interest you."

Boudija paused, waiting for his code name to be recognized and for his words to sink in. "It would be worthwhile talking about it tonight. Let's say at your place in an hour and a half."

Chapter Eleven

Lieutenant-Colonel Bikbashi Fuad Abdul Nasser was a heavy and ponderous man. His neck was thick, his hands were thick, and his belly was thick—and sagging. His gait was elephantine, his movements at first glance seemed slow and clumsy. But in spite of appearances, the special assistant to the Egyptian ambassador to France had a sharp brain and his reactions were totally out of character with his physical appearance.

It is true—and he was the first to admit it—that being cousin to the Egyptian ruler Gamal Abdul Nasser had helped him in his career. Being made a key man in the security service of his country had not required any special talent on his part. Once established in his post, however, he showed that he was ambitious and diligent, and he became outstandingly successful at his job.

In Paris he became the nerve center of Egyptian counterintelligence for all of Europe. He also served as contact man for other security services. His specialty was kidnapping enemy agents or opponents of his cousin; after drugging them, he arranged for their transportation to the land of the Nile.

It was early in November, 1968. Fuad was sitting in the study of the substantial building that served as his "after hours" headquarters. It was in reality the center of operations of the Egyptian intelligence agency in the French capital. The guards outside had been carefully posted and were totally invisible to anyone peering through the front gates.

A taxi drew up; the driver looked doubtfully at the house, which was in total darkness, and said to his passenger: "Are you sure this is the right place? There doesn't appear to be anybody home. There are no taxis in this neighborhood. If necessary, I can wait a few minutes for you." Colonel Habib Boudija shook his head. He paid his fare, and the taxi drove off.

The Moroccan looked around him. His professional training showed in the way his eyes swept the surrounding area to see if he had been followed. Automatically he soaked in the details of the house. The large metal gate. The asphalt path. The high wall. The total isolation of the two-story building. The Egyptian secret service man had chosen his base of operations well. It was a mere fifteen-minute taxi ride from the center of Paris, yet the tall trees and the location made the premises an ideal espionage center.

Boudija walked confidently toward the entrance. Out of the corner of his eye he discerned a figure partially hidden by the shadows next to the stone wall just to the right of the gate. He stopped, lit a cigarette, and waited until the guard approached him. As he had anticipated, he did not have long to wait.

A large man, his face dark and sharp-featured, approached and stopped a few feet from the Moroccan. With one hand casually tucked inside his jacket, he asked: "Mr. Boudija?"

"Yes."

The guard now came closer and said: "Please forgive me for treating a guest like this, but I am obliged to make a short body-search. I have orders, you understand . . ."

The guard's practiced hands ran rapidly down and then up again from head to toe. His touch was light and impersonal, but Habib Boudija recognized the skill of a true professional.

"If you are ever in need of a job, come and see me," he said with a smile.

"Thank you, sir," the guard replied, obviously flattered. He was well aware of the awesome reputation of the Moroccan intelligence chief.

As they walked across the well-kept lawn, the Moroccan saw that the house was fairly new and, observing the way that it was situated on the grounds, he realized that it could have been built expressly for its present purpose. Boudija had once tried to persuade General Muhammed Ofkir that he could use a similar setup tucked into a few acres of woodland and garden, just like the "Egyptian place" as he termed it. The idea had been turned down because of the expense.

They entered the building through a thick oak door. The strong light that struck Boudija full in the face as he stepped indoors was not visible from the road because of the wooden shutters and heavy red velvet curtains. He had to blink hard before he realized that Fuad Abdul Nasser was standing right in front of him, a welcoming smile on his broad face.

The two men embraced. They were extremely close even though there had been "differences of opinion" between their respective governments. Indeed, at that very moment, the Egyptian president was engaged in a scheme to kill the Moroccan king. But here in Paris between professionals there were no hard feelings about such matters. Nasser and Boudija really did like one another.

For some time they gossiped idly as they consumed several cups of thick Turkish coffee. Finally they got down to business.

"The Israelis want to buy a shipment of uranium that we have acquired for industrial purposes."

The second part of this announcement was not quite accurate, as the Egyptian knew full well, but he let it pass. The Moroccans had no need of nuclear raw material; the uranium had been intended to be sold to the Indians at an enormous profit.

Boudija went on. "The Israelis are desperate. France has closed the uranium tap to them. The Americans are not willing to give them any uranium either, without the right to inspect that mysterious nuclear reactor of theirs at

110

Dimona. The Israelis are not anxious for the Americans, or anybody else for that matter, to see what they are up to there. We can guess for ourselves actually. The Israelis are being pressed from all sides. They need the uranium badly."

So far, Fuad had learned nothing new. He was fully aware of the Moroccan's deal with the Indians. There were a lot of loose tongues in New Delhi, and bribery was a way of life there. It was well known that you could buy any information you wanted for only a few dollars. In fact, the Indians came running with information, from the lowest clerks right up to the highest government officials.

The Egyptian listened carefully. He knew some kind of deal was going to be proposed. It had not been the first time that the Moroccan had turned up with some "information" that he was ready to sell for Swiss francs deposited to his account—always in advance. The intelligence service of several countries knew that Boudija was ready to sell his mother if he could get some quick cash in exchange. With a smile to himself, Fuad realized that he even knew the man's private account number in Zurich by heart. This was quite deliberate, this mental storing away of useful information. There might come a time when it was necessary to "lean" on his friend—and what better instrument of blackmail than his private banking affairs.

The Moroccan waited while Fuad thought for a few moments. "How much do you want?" he finally asked.

Obviously the colonel was about to make a deal with the Israelis and double-cross the Indians. Now he was going to carry out a double, double-cross. He was offering the Egyptians the uranium cargo.

"The Israelis have offered me ten percent of the value of the material. That is three hundred and fifty thousand dollars. I could arrange things so that they don't get it, and it could be sent instead to Alexandria."

"Four hundred thousand?"

The Moroccan looked unenthusiastic.

"Four hundred and fifty thousand?"

Boudija stood up.

"It's a deal."

The Egyptian rose slowly from his armchair. "I'll need

confirmation from my chiefs in Cairo. You know without my saying so that this is an important matter and a lot of money. I will give you my reply in twenty-four hours. But frankly, between you and me, I see no problem. As soon as I have received confirmation we can get down to discussing details."

Thomas Green, captain of the freighter *Dominic*, was directing "sea-clear work," the final preparations before sailing. His destination was Antwerp, as it had been on dozens of previous occasions. He was as eager as his crew to be leaving Pointe Noire after taking on a load of crude uranium ore from Shaba Province in Zaire. He hated spending much time in the unbearably humid climate of tropical Africa and neither he nor his crew, most of whom were also English, cared for black women.

When the ship got underway, the ocean was perfectly calm, as it can be only in the tropics. That had been reason enough for deciding to sail for Europe several hours earlier than planned, a decision that cheered the skipper considerably.

Captain Thomas Green was a man of medium height, with thick tattooed arms. His face was scarred, but he never spoke about the incident that had resulted in his being so marked for life. He was totally indifferent as to the cargo his ship was carrying for the Belgian Société Générale des Minerais. He simply did a job, and did it well and efficiently. He was looking forward to being in Antwerp in thirteen days' time.

On the 7th of November, 1968, at 8:30 in the morning, Colonel Habib Boudija telephoned Mike and in a guarded conversation let it be known that General Muhammed Ofkir approved of the financial details of the uranium deal which would settle accounts between them. They arranged to meet at the corner of Avenue Waterloo and Avenue Louis, in a small bar that had served as a rendezvous in the past. On Mike's insistence, the colonel had come to Belgium.

The Moroccan now pressed Mike for details, details of how he planned to operate once he got the uranium, but the Mossad man was evasive. He leaned across the table and, lightly touching Habib's arm, said: "The less you know the better it is for you and the general, and the fewer the lies you will have to tell to different people later on."

Mike was watching the face of the Moroccan closely. An instinct warned him of trouble, yet he continued as though nothing were wrong.

"A ship, the *Scheersberg A*, will load the barrels of uranium in Antwerp. We know who the official owners are. We also have details on the crew. Not one of them is Moroccan. I would be most pleased if you could arrange for two of your people to join the crew. Because of the special nature of the cargo I am sure that could be easily explained."

The Moroccan looked at the Mossad commander suspiciously, but Mike went on hurriedly: "Really, there is no problem and nothing to be worried about. It would be totally consistent with the situation for you to explain that in view of the danger of Israeli agents becoming too interested in the cargo you want to insure proper protection for the whole crew. You could even offer to pay the wages of the two men you put on board. That would make it even more acceptable to the captain."

The colonel was quick to get the point. "Spell out what you want. The *last* thing you really want are two of my men getting in your hair!"

Mike grinned. "I would consider the account settled to the last line if you could let me have two sets of original Moroccan seamen's papers. Properly stamped. I will arrange for them to be picked up in Marseilles."

The colonel paused for a second or two. "You'll have to give me photographs of the two men."

Now Mike's mental warning bells were ringing loud and clear. He knew the colonel was devious and had a mind as twisted as the tail of a donkey, as the Arab saying went. There was something about his behavior that made Mike trust him even less than usual.

In any event, even if the situation was one hundred percent safe, he was not going to risk the lives of two of his best men—one of whom was his closest friend.

"I'll see to it that you get the photographs . . . in Marseilles," said Mike evenly. "I will send someone to wherever you say. You can give him the documents. You will show him where to put the photographs. And your part will end right there. No more demands from me. We are all square."

The colonel forced a smile. "Thanks for trusting me!"

The two men rose.

"I'll let you know where the meeting place is," said the Moroccan.

They parted without shaking hands.

Chapter Twelve

The small classified advertisement "Garage for Sale" in the Antwerp newspaper was one of dozens appearing in the "Property and Business" column, so Emile Golder was a little startled to receive a telephone call so promptly. The man who had spotted the notice dismissed Golder's suggestion that he come and look at the place in person. "We don't want to waste each other's time," he said in a businesslike way. "I would like to know the precise size. Its height, width, the dimensions of the doors, as well as what equipment is available."

Emile Golder realized that he was speaking to a foreigner but could not place the light accent. He could sense, however, that the man was genuinely interested in the place, and the Belgian began to feel very relieved. The reason for his delight in finding a prospective customer was simply that the garage was situated in a down-at-the-heels area of the city that was, if anything, becoming bleaker day by day. It was scheduled for redevelopment some time in the future, but no one seemed to know quite when.

Golder was an excellent mechanic, but when he had inherited the garage from his father, also in the same trade, he realized that he would never make a living there. It was in the wrong place. Customers were few and far between. For two years real estate agents had tried to sell it for him but had not succeeded in finding a single customer. Somebody had then suggested that he try and rent it out. At least that way he could derive some income until such time as a customer for purchase came along. Here within hours of the advertisement appearing was a serious-sounding caller!

The mechanic was an honest man, and he suddenly cut in as the caller was putting more and more questions to him: "I think I must tell you that trade in the area for a commercial garage is not exactly brilliant. But of course it is going cheap . . ."

This did not seem to bother the foreigner in the slightest. Perhaps the man was thinking of converting it into a bonded warehouse, like a lot of the other buildings in the area. The mechanic remembered that when he was a boy it was a place where people lived. Then, gradually, the houses gave way to businesses and shops, and now it was a district of warehouses. The area was dismal and lonely; people were hardly ever seen in the streets any more. It was for this reason that Emile Golder had had to move out with his family and start up a small business in another part of Antwerp. He was making a good living, but some income, or better still some capital, would be a godsend.

One hour later, two men arrived in a gray Peugeot 404. One had thick, flaxen hair. Emile could see immediately that he was the professional. The other was a queer kind of fish. He did not say anything and he had a long, expressionless face—the sort of person a man like himself did not know how to handle. Emile felt uncomfortable every time he glanced in his direction.

The professional examined the garage minutely. In particular, he scrutinized the locks on the main door and rear door. Then he tried out the hoisting equipment; Emile quickly explained: "That hasn't been used for some time. But it works, I assure you. All it needs is a little bit of maintenance work. In fact, I'll do it for you. It will only take me an hour or two."

The two men made no comment. They looked at the

grease pit and the air pressure pump, which Emile knew *was* working. He had checked it before the arrival of the two potential buyers.

They measured the garage by pacing out steps, and carefully estimated the height of the ceiling as well as the thickness of the walls. Emile tried his best to play the role of salesman: "You can see this place was built in the days when they really knew how to build," he said proudly. The flaxen-haired man politely silenced him. He was making up his own mind and didn't need any help in making his calculations.

As he watched, the mechanic tried to figure out where the men came from. "One looked like a Swede," he was to explain afterward. "The other was of Mediterranean origin, but I couldn't tell from where. He hardly said a word."

To his intense delight, the professional, as the mechanic had labeled him, said: "I would like to rent the place for a trial period of three months. I know that there's not much business around here. You were right! It's more like a graveyard than a city! But we'll give it a try and we'll talk again in a few months' time. In the meantime I'll give cash for three months' rent. Perhaps you can give me a receipt."

"If you don't mind me mentioning it, are you going to declare this payment to the authorities?" the mechanic asked cautiously. "You understand that it makes a difference as far as my tax is concerned."

"It will be a perfectly private matter between the two of us," the flaxen-haired man said solemnly.

At 6:30 that night an orange-colored Scania trailer truck turned into the dark and deserted street. Only one of the dozen streetlights was in working order. The vehicle, which carried a large blue container, twenty feet in length, drew up cautiously alongside the front door of the garage. A man jumped out, unlocked the garage door and signaled the driver to give him a hand in opening the large wooden doors as wide as possible.

With his lights extinguished, and guided only by the voice of his companion, the driver carefully backed the truck into the garage. It was not easy, and he cursed as

117

the side mirror caught against a post and was nearly ripped off. No sooner was the truck inside than the wooden garage doors were closed.

Ten minutes later the gray Peugeot 404 turned into the street and parked some distance away from the garage. Two men got out and walked slowly down the dark, uneven surface of the cobblestone street. The district, one of the oldest and most neglected of the city, was not far from the harbor area, as the smell of the sea and dead fish indicated. Tonight not a soul was about.

Suddenly a black Citroën drew up at the other end of the street. Seated inside were a couple—a dark-haired woman and a blond man. They sat for a few minutes without exchanging a single word. Then, at a signal from the truck driver, they both opened their doors simultaneously and walked toward the garage. They joined the two men from the Peugeot and together the group went through the rotting wooden door at the right-hand side of the garage.

One man remained on guard there, peering at the street through a crack until he made sure they had not been observed. No one was around. Even so, the guard remained where he was, watching the street, while the others made their way to the rear of the run-down garage.

The four men greeted each other warmly and amiably slapped shoulders as old and trusted friends do when meeting after a long separation.

Then one after the other, they went over to the tall black-haired woman and brushed lips against her cheek. Ze'ev Biran, Ruby Goldman, Gad Ullman, Benny Arnheim—she knew them all. The pale light of the single naked bulb dangling from a long cord from the ceiling gave Sharon Manners's pretty face a look of mystery. Her eyes were shining with suppressed excitement as each called her by her name and kissed her. All of them were well aware that although they had been on operations before, either separately or in groups, this time they were working on something very special indeed.

Mike leaned back against the office desk covered with piles of oily paper. With a grimace, Sharon sat down on a wooden bench after removing a large handkerchief from her bag and covering the soiled seat. The others were less fussy. They sat where they could. One even used an up-side-down oil drum as a stool. It was the first occasion they had all been brought together.

"From now on you all know with whom you are working," Mike said by way of introduction. "And in a few moments you will also know why you are here."

He spoke slowly, in short, clipped sentences; it was as though he was imitating the lectures he had received from Professor Benjamin Bentheim. He outlined the grave situation of the nuclear reactor at Dimona, faced with total paralysis as a result of General de Gaulle's embargo.

"We must see to it that the reactor does not run out of fuel. For reasons that we needn't go into, Sharon was taken into my confidence earlier than the rest of you. Through her good services we know about the movements of uranium shipments into and throughout Europe. We also have precise information on the destinations of these cargoes and the quantities involved."

There was a sudden whistle of surprise from the man seated on Mike's left. "Piracy at sea! I should have guessed right from the beginning!"

Mike turned to him. "Ze'ev," he said, "I knew you hadn't lost your cunning. Imagine telling me you are too old for this sort of thing! Yes, you've got the basic idea. But don't worry. You are in no danger of losing your captain's license if you get caught. For the simple reason that you are not going to get caught. We just can't afford it." This was Mike at his best. His supreme self-confidence was contagious and bolstered the morale of his squad.

Mike pointed to the container. "Over the next six days you'll have to make this box your living quarters. Inside are welding tools and other equipment. There is also a communications system. There is food and air-conditioning. And special arrangements for the calls of nature. You can change things around to suit yourselves. You are to stay there for three days before there's any action. Of course you have already understood that you are going to be handled as cargo and loaded aboard a ship. Two of our men will join the vessel posing as crew. Their role is to release you from the container. Once that is done, you will take over the ship by seizing it the way pirates used to do in the old days."

Then Mike got down to the precise technical details of the operation, all of which had been worked out step by step at headquarters. For several hours they went over the carefully prepared and timed mission, each expert pointing out any weak spots as they occurred to him.

The tools to be carried out were divided among the group. Hours later, Sharon left the building with Mike, the blond man who had rented the garage. They went out by the back door while two of the others left by the front. The two who remained behind opened the container door, lowered the upholstered benches, which were bolted onto its walls, and promptly went to sleep.

*The exterior measurements of the container were: 6.05 meters long, by 2.44 meters wide, by 2.44 meters high. The interior measurements were: 5.92 meters by 2.36 meters by 2.25 meters.

Chapter Thirteen

Two dark-skinned men wearing duffel coats and roll-neck shirts left the central railway station in Marseilles. They carried battered suitcases that had obviously seen better days. The men were unmistakably sailors, which was hardly odd since this was one of the busiest ports in the Mediterranean. They walked for a short while, then took a cab, giving the driver an address near the old harbor, not far from the casbah.

The driver was quick. Minutes later, the two men ended up a mile away, just off the Quai du Port on the old harbor, at a restaurant specializing in bouillabaisse. They ordered this delicacy, followed by *fruits de la mer*, and to help wash down the excellent meal they chose a bottle of dry white wine. As they were completing their main course, a waiter with a lean, lined face appeared at their table.

"May I recommend the *crème caramel?*" he asked with a nicotine-stained smile. From his accent it was clear that he was not a native of Marseilles. The two men glanced up at him sharply. They nodded their heads, affirming the order, and a few minutes later the waiter returned holding a silver tray. On it were two dishes filled with dessert. As he lowered the tray to the table he pretended to be having trouble balancing it. As he righted it, he dropped a bulging envelope into the lap of the older of the two men. The incident passed unnoticed by the other diners.

The older man, who until very recently had worked in Tel Aviv as a Mossad Special Operations Division instructor, was known to his apprentice agents as Meir Azoulai. His companion, Shauli Mizrachi, came from the Arab affairs department of the same organization. Meir opened the envelope and examined its contents with great interest.

It contained two cards in green plastic folders. They were seamen's papers bearing the official stamp of the Moroccan Ministry of the Interior. They were blank, and it would be an easy task to fill in whatever names were deemed necessary. The colonel of the Moroccan intelligence service in Paris had fulfilled his part of the deal.

The waiter arrived with the bill. Meir's eyes opened wide at what he considered the inflated price of the food he had just eaten, but he settled the bill without saying a word. Orders were orders.

The two men left the restaurant and walked slowly toward the old harbor. The shorter of the two glanced at his watch. They had two hours to kill before they had to catch the fast train to Paris. They turned toward the casbah area.

It was broad daylight, but the narrow dark alleys that separated the filthy old buildings were crowded. A group of Greek sailors went past noisily and approached a seedy hotel at whose entrance sat three whores wrapped in artificial mink. For several minutes they stood arguing about the price in a mixture of broken English and French. Finally an agreement was reached and, laughing loudly, the group went upstairs.

The two men with the Moroccan seamen's papers in their pockets walked slowly up the steep street between rows of houses. Prostitutes of all colors and ages gave them the come-on in a dozen languages. Five swarthy men, Moroccans or Algerians, crowded around a rigged-up gambling table, throwing dice. One of the men called out to the two passers-by to join them. The invitation was declined.

As the two men came to a crossroad that was almost deserted, a Mercedes pulled across in front of them. Three men burst out simultaneously before the car had even come to a halt. They held Berettas with silencers attached. The driver sat immobile behind the wheel, keeping the engine running.

For a split second the eyes of the two sailors met. Then, as if at a single unspoken command, they leaped backward.

The five dice-throwers blocked their way. Three of them held short-bladed knives. The other two had revolvers.

It all happened very quickly, as passers-by later told the police. The ring of men closed in on the two sailors. They tried climbing the wall of a house which stood on the east side of the street. Two of their assailants jumped in front of them. They were now at arms' length from each other. The taller of the sailors turned suddenly and landed a kick of stunning power in the face of one of the attackers. The crack of breaking bone could be heard clearly in the narrow street. The man dropped his knife with a cry.

The second sailor kicked out too. He drove his foot powerfully between the legs of the man nearest him. The man dropped to the ground as though he had been struck by lightning. Turning on his heel he struck out again with his foot. This time he made contact with an attacker's chest. But before he could strike again, he was hit on the head with a heavy object and fell to the cobblestones.

The tall man tried to reach the knife that had fallen. He almost succeeded. His fingers were inches away when a kick landed right in his ribs. He turned and again made for the wall of the nearby house.

There was a shadow behind him. Turning, he welcomed the attacker with a sharply raised knee. The blow struck home hard and true. The assailant fell clutching his lower belly in agony. With the speed of light, the tall man leaped at him and grabbed the Beretta from his hands. He steadied the weapon quickly and fired into the stomach of the attacker nearest him. The gun made a faint plopping sound. The man fell to the ground, but in so doing he clutched at the sailor, nearly dragging him down.

Again the sailor tried to fire. But before he could squeeze the trigger, something struck him in the chest. The force of the blow sent him backward. His head struck the wall he had been trying to reach. A heavy foot trod into his face, and he took no further part in the fight.

The police were told that the two men had been swiftly picked up off the pavement and flung into the car. The dead attacker and those injured were carried into a nearby alleyway, while the Mercedes rocketed off with a scream of tires.

Chapter Fourteen

The artist sitting behind the easel on the protected side of the warehouse had had quite a job getting permission to set up his canvases in Antwerp's dock area. Finally, after closely examining his identity papers, an indulgent police officer shrugged his shoulders and said: "You understand that you go there at your own risk. It is quite dangerous. There are a lot of cranes and many trucks driving around. I also ask you to observe all the regulations in the area."

Despite his official stance, the police officer had a soft spot for painters. He had wanted to be an artist himself, but his strict parents had quickly disabused him of the idea of "wasting his time at art school." So he had joined the police force instead.

The artist with his black beret and moustache, his faded denims and paint-stained smock, thanked the officer profusely. "I am hoping to get my canvases displayed in an exhibition in a month's time. The sea has always fascinated me; I love the vitality of the dockyards—the vessels at work, the loading and unloading, the faces of the dockers and stevedores." Expressing gratitude for his help, the artist took down the officer's home address and promised to send him an invitation to the opening.

Now he was working with frantic speed. To the curious passer-by who bothered to stop and stare, he explained that he liked to make a lot of rough sketches before he actually got down to working in oil on canvas. Unquestionably he was diligent. He came early in the morning and only packed his possessions in an old bag when the light had faded from the evening sky. Finally, using color liberally, he began to paint canvas after canvas.

He drew dockers and ships and cranes. He seemed particularly fascinated by shed number 17. From where he was sitting he could see every bale and container inside the large building. He also painted the long wharf, right up to the oil terminal. Sometimes he even used a pair of binoculars he had brought along to get a better view of the subjects he was putting on canvas.

On the 16th of November he worked with particular speed. This was the day that the *Scheersberg A* arrived from Rotterdam. That evening the artist left earlier than usual.

He never returned. The only one who noticed that he no longer came was the police officer who had wanted to be an artist. And later, he wondered why he never received the promised invitation to the exhibition.

Not far away in a garage behind locked doors, two technicians were carefully fixing one of the artist's paintings into a container now loaded onto a large Scania truck. The vehicle had originally been orange-colored, but now it was a dark maroon. Its license plates had also been changed. There was no other car or truck in the garage. In the corner of the office at the back of the building stood a pile of rejected oil paintings. They portrayed stevedores, cranes, ships, and other sights that can be found in any modern dock yard anywhere in the world.

For over two hours five men pored over a particular drawing which the artist had prepared for them. Again and again they went over the operation, step by step, trying to eliminate every weak point and anticipate every possible unexpected emergency. Now and then the artist looked at the neglected and abandoned canvases. "Some of them," he thought to himself, "are pretty good, even if I say so myself!"

Thirty-six hours earlier, hundreds of miles away, in another closely guarded room in the bustling seaport of Marseilles, another group of men were gathered. One was Bikbashi Fuad Abdul Nasser, the Egyptian secret service chief for all of Europe. With him was Colonel Habib Boudija, his Moroccan counterpart. In their hands they held the two green plastic folders containing Moroccan seamen's papers which had been delivered earlier in the day to the two Mossad operators.

It was later established that there were two other men in the room as well. They were trained "heavies"—trained in the art of torture by the Moroccan colonel. He in turn had had for a "professor" in the subject his superior, General Muhammed Ofkir, the same Ofkir who had learned all that there was to know about torture from the Viet Cong. Both Ofkir and Boudija were convinced that they had improved the techniques they had learned from each successive set of masters.

The two Mossad agents had been brutally tortured. Meir Azoulai died without saying a word. The younger, less experienced man, Shauli, did break, as it turned out. He revealed some secrets. Then he was shot—a coup de grace, for he was by then close to death anyway.

Chapter Fifteen

Thomas Green hated docking so far from the main gate of the port—not just in Antwerp—in any port. It meant a long walk, particularly at night, after enjoying the pleasures of the city, but there was nothing he could do about it. The *Dominic* invariably had to make her way to isolated spots; her special cargo of uranium was always unloaded on out-of-the-way and well-guarded wharves. The heavy lead barrels in which the uranium ore was packed were awkward and bulky. But Green knew that the yellowish material had to be kept this way in order to protect him and his crew from radiation.

"I wonder about the poor bastards who dig the stuff out of the ground," he thought. "Does anyone worry about *their* health problems?" He dismissed the question as quickly as it came; his job was to bring the material to Europe.

He stood watching the barrels being loaded rapidly from the platforms into the railroad cars of the Euratom supply agency. He knew that the sealed cars of the goods train went from the military dock to underground depots at an army base not far from Brussels. Shipments went out from the base to atomic reactors all over Europe. One of

the drivers had once told him that this base was among
the most heavily guarded areas in the entire country.
"They keep an eye on the stuff as though it was more precious than gold," was the man's comment.

Sometimes, however, the process varied; the barrels of
uranium were loaded onto sealed trucks, which also belonged to the Euratom agency, and were then taken to
other parts of the dock area and loaded onto waiting ships.
This was the case with the cargo on the 16th of November, 1968.

The long trucks with the emblem of the Euratom supply
agency painted on their sides came in one after the other.
Each in turn swallowed up its ration of the precious
uranium in squat barrels and then moved off in a convoy
to cargo dock 33-West. Here the working lights on the
deck of the German-built freighter *Scheersberg A*, registered with Lloyds of London as a vessel of 1,790 gross
tons, and flying the Liberian flag, had already been lit before the barrels of uranium began to arrive. Euratom security men, as well as dock-yard agents, kept a close eye
on the vessel. Every additional truck that arrived only
served to strengthen the heavy security net thrown around
the ship. In the cabin of every truck sat an armed guard
with orders to shoot if attacked.

The *Scheersberg A* swung gently on her hawsers. She
had two holds with her superstructure aft. She was 260
feet long and capable of traveling at a steady 12 knots.
There were many vessels like her that plied the length and
breadth of the English Channel, but she seemed to be in
worse shape than most.

The run-down appearance of the *Scheersberg A* made
her look much older than her thirteen years. Large rust
patches covered the cargo deck, which at one time had
been painted gray. The sides of the ship had not been
treated to a fresh protective coat of paint for many
months, and they, too, were covered with large stains. The
superstructure and the bridge were a pale, faded orange,
and the funnel, which had originally been orange with a
black stripe around its base, was now almost entirely
blackened with soot. Little wonder that Hamburg ship-
broker August Bolten had been pleased to sell the ship to
the mysterious "Middle-Eastern or Oriental gentleman"

who had pulled German bank notes totaling slightly less than $300,000 out of a briefcase to buy the ship on behalf of the Biscayne Traders Shipping Corporation.

The first officer, Barney MacDowell, strode the length of the deck examining its poorly maintained equipment which was lying around in an untidy and chaotic mess. Theoretically the vessel was to have gone into drydock for refitting before this particular journey, but obviously he had been misinformed and it had not. "There's going to be a real revolution here before I'm finished," he muttered to himself. "There's going to be a reign of terror and some discipline instilled into the work habits of this lot." While he was on the subject of change, he also decided that if he had his way the entire crew would be replaced as well.

MacDowell's posting on the *Scheersberg* had been totally by chance. He had been registered at the employment office of the sea-officers club in Glasgow for four months before the job on the German-built ship had cropped up. He had never heard of the company that owned the ship—the Biscayne Traders Shipping Corporation.

When he arrived aboard the vessel at Antwerp, after leaving Rotterdam the previous day, he was told simply that the owner was a man called Fritz Kopke. The crew were a mixture of Spaniards, Austrians, Greeks, and Indians. The captain, who was introduced to him as Peter Barrow, was very young, in his mid-twenties. The second officer was a Greek with an unpronounceable surname. He was called Christos—and that is the only name Barney MacDowell knew him by. There were also three ship's engineers whose origins seemed vague, and three motor-men, either Greek or Cypriot, who worked in the engine room.

MacDowell was not happy about the fact that the owners had chosen to load the ship with the night shift. It meant an extra working night for him, and he hated the prospect, particularly in a lively city like Antwerp. The long, sealed trucks on the wharf gradually built up into a well-organized and orderly line. The hatches of holds one and two had been opened well in advance, ready for loading.

MacDowell had to personally supervise the careful transfer of the heavy lead barrels and several large containers into the ship's hold. He realized with some disappointment that there would be no chance of shore leave for him that night. Sailing time was already posted on the off-duty list: 6:00 A.M. According to his calculations, this meant that they would be in Genoa in about nine days' time.

The loading of the 560 barrels, on whose sides the word "plumbat" was clearly marked, got underway at a very slow pace. The dock workers seemed to resent so many guards keeping an eye on them and they worked at half speed. Even the tally check seemed unnecessarily complicated for such a simple cargo. Finally, at ten minutes to midnight, the job was finished. Worn out, First Officer Barney MacDowell turned in for a few hours' sleep before sailing.

Not far away, in the garage with the heavy wooden doors, the last-minute preparations on the container which was to serve as a home were being completed. The outside had been hastily repainted red and now the last of the welding equipment and the communications complex as well as adequate supplies of food and water and other necessary items were carefully tied down.

Mike's black Citroën pulled up in front of the garage. Gad Ullman sat next to him. He had acted as the Mossad commander's shadow at the hurried meeting that the Moroccan contact had unexpectedly demanded a mere three hours before. Mike had not liked this unexpected turn of events. He much preferred it when *he* was the one who made arrangements for any rendezvous, particularly when dealing with agents of another security service.

Colonel Habib Boudija's request to see him face to face once more, right here in Antwerp, aroused an uneasy sense of suspicion about the Moroccan's motives. The colonel said he had changed his mind about the handling of payments. He did not want the $350,000 bribe paid into his account, as previously arranged; he wanted it in cash.

This struck Mike as odd. In the world of espionage there was no room for failing to meet a commitment. At the top level, which is where they were now dealing, they were all professionals, and professional men kept their word. In the international intelligence community even a suggestion that an individual might be "untrustworthy" meant that no one would ever deal with him again. In addition, his future life expectancy would not be too good either. Mike knew this, and he was well aware that the colonel knew the rules too. Nonetheless, his feelings of anxiety increased minute by minute.

Mike had been waiting at a table in the Café Papillon for five minutes when Colonel Habib Boudija came in. They spoke for only a short time and then Mike pushed the suitcase that had been resting between his legs toward the Moroccan. The colonel signaled that all was well, and Mike got up and left.

On the way to the garage he took several extra turns at the last minute, constantly changing his speed, while Gad Ullman never took his eyes off the back window to make sure that they were not being followed. Only when Mike was absolutely certain that they were clear did he pull into the quiet and deserted street where his squad was waiting for him.

He drove into the garage and parked his car beside the truck. By the time he had left his seat, the large wooden doors, moving silently on their recently greased and repaired hinges, were closed. The man on guard at the entrance reported that there had been no unusual movement. The street was like a graveyard. It was dark now—the night of November 16, 1968.

The team knew that they had to leave the garage in exactly one hour. In accordance with the loading timetable of the ship, the port gate had to be reached by 7:30 that night.

Mike called everyone into the garage office. In addition to the four men who made up the "pirate" takeover unit, there were two others. One was the truck driver and the other was his mate. Without his toothbrush moustache, long-haired wig, the French beret, he no longer looked like an artist with a passion for painting ships and dockers—in great haste but with no particular talent.

Once again they went over the details of the operation. Then the final preparations for loading the container were carefully checked and rechecked. Mike looked at his watch. Twenty minutes to go before they had to set off.

Benny Arnheim, the perfectionist, had decided to synchronize his instrument "just once more to make absolutely sure." This remark brought a smile to the faces of his tense companions. If anyone in this world prepared himself thoroughly for an operation, it was the "radio genius," as they called him. The very possibility that his equipment could ever dare to be out of order seemed preposterous.

Suddenly the fingers of the radio operator froze as he toyed with one of the terminals. He moved the knob gently with the delicacy of a master violinist drawing the ultimate in tonal quality from the instrument cradled under his chin. He touched the various buttons in quick succession, then without a word got up from his wooden seat in the container. He jumped off the truck and began to walk slowly along its length, checking every screw.

The others watched him in puzzlement. They saw him walk over to Mike's Citroën and peer inside, opening each door in turn. He raised the hood, then suddenly got down on his hands and knees and looked under the body of the car. A smile of satisfaction spread across his face and he eased his way under the rear end of the vehicle.

Out of sight of the others, he stretched out his fingers and carefully wrapped them around a curved metallic object. With a sudden jerk, he wrenched something off the metal bodywork of the car. Benny slid out from under the Citroën, and, moving into the light, closely examined the object he had found.

It was an ellipse-shaped instrument; one side was flat so that it could be attached to a metal body, like that of a car. Benny Arnheim did not have to examine it for more than a second or two to know exactly what it was he had discovered beneath the Citroën, nor was it the first time that he had detected similar instruments—or for that matter, made good use of them himself on several missions.

It was a miniature transmitter, a direction finder—a gadget widely used by intelligence services the world over. Someone sitting somewhere, perhaps not very far away, had tracked Mike right to this very spot in the lonely garage not far from the docks in Antwerp.

Benny Arnheim ran to Mike's office where the Mossad commander was taking one last look at a detailed map of the harbor area, and in particular the precise position of the docks. The radio operator did not have to waste time explaining the purpose of the instrument in his hand.

"Where did you find it?" Mike asked curtly.

"It was stuck under your tail," came the reply.

The Mossad chief crashed his fist onto the table and cursed. "That bastard! That was the reason for that last visit . . ." It was the first time that Benny had ever seen Mike lose control. The emotional outburst was over in a second. The professional commander, ready for action, swept aside his fury, not only at being outsmarted by the Moroccan but also for the man's act of betrayal. What else was Colonel Habib Boudija up to?

Mike rose swiftly to his feet. He sent the truckdriver to the door of the garage to reinforce the man on duty there. Then, in a calm, decisive voice he told the squad: "I am expecting visitors. They should be here at any minute. Let's get ready for them. Immediately."

The driver's voice cut in: "We won't have long to wait. They are already outside."

Almost before the words were out of the man's mouth, Mike, moving like a panther preparing to pounce on his prey, was standing beside his lookouts. Through a wide crack at the side of the entrance he could see a number of shadows. They were making their way silently and expertly in a line along the wall of houses on the opposite side of the narrow street. They took up positions at the entrance to the building. A black Mercedes stood parked about sixty-five feet to the right of the entrance, its lights extinguished. It was difficult in the dark to count the number of men, but from the shadows Mike guessed that the ambush consisted of at least six persons.

Mike retraced his steps slowly toward the center of the garage. His head was bowed. The squad of Mossad operators knew he was working out a plan of action. They were all armed and ready. In their hands they held either Berettas with silencers or Uzi machine guns, also equipped with silencers.

Without moving his lips, using only swift gestures, Mike gave them their orders. His movements were quick and economical. Every man knew exactly what to do. The driver got into the cab and released the brake gently, so as not to make a sound. The doors of the container were shut. Two men stood by the doors of the garage ready to swing them open.

Gad Ullman and Mike took up positions on the vehicle between the cab of the truck and the container. They held Uzis. Two others climbed a ladder to the upper floor of the garage and eased their way beside the darkened windows which looked down into the street below.

The wooden doors swung open as the driver started the engine with a roar. The truck moved forward slowly. The driver was invisible in the dark as he pressed the accelerator, the other foot on the brake. The headlights of the truck were on full as though it was heading directly for the wall opposite the garage.

The shooting started as the wheels touched the stone pavement on the other side of the street. Bullets flew in all directions. The vehicle stopped moving, its engine died. Bullets sprayed the driver's cab. There was a tinkle of breaking glass. Apart from the soft whine of bullets and the thud of impact when they struck wood or metal, the shooting was soundless.

From his "command post" behind the cab, Mike offered up a quick little prayer of thanks that on this occasion the other side also employed professionals. Like his own men, they were using revolvers and automatic weapons fitted with silencers. No one wanted the Belgian police to come running to see what was happening.

From the direction of the shots, it was clear that the attackers had taken cover in the entrances of the three buildings opposite the garage. They were also stationed at an angle to it behind the parked Mercedes.

Mike and Gad Ullman, well hidden behind the driver's cab, were protected by plates of solid metal. Just behind the hood of the Mercedes, Mike spotted a man aiming a Kalashnikov sub-machine gun at the garage entrance. The man obviously expected to see fleeing figures emerge from the building at any second. The Mossad commander turned the barrel of his Uzi in the direction of the ambusher and squeezed the trigger. The man involuntarily threw his weapon upward. With a sharp cry he collapsed onto the hood and gently, as if in slow motion, slithered to the ground.

Gad Ullman did not wait long before taking action. He

could not identify any particular target so he opened fire on the entrance of the building on his right. It was like a gunfight in a silent movie. Only the shouts of the wounded, the noise of striking bullets, and men's feet on the cobblestones and pavement could be heard.

Now Ze'ev Biran and Ruby were in the thick of it. From their positions on the upper floor of the garage they let fly a murderous barrage. Unable to see precise targets in the dark, they directed their fire at the entrances of the buildings opposite the garage. These were the positions *they* would have taken up had it been their role to be the attackers.

The second man behind the Mercedes spotted Mike. He fired without hesitating a second. A burning sensation seared the Mossad commander's cheek. Steadying himself by leaning against the cab, Mike pulled the trigger of his Uzi. His entire burst missed its target, and the man retreated toward the rear of the car where a hail of bullets were poured into his body by a Mossad agent who had spotted him from behind the truck. It was one of the men who had opened the garage doors and who was now in the thick of the shooting.

From the way the attackers were now behaving, they seemed to have prepared no alternative plan of action. It was becoming clear to Mike that they had banked on storming the building, taking it totally by surprise. They had not taken into account the possibility of being shot at before they were ready to leap into action.

"Typical," Mike thought. "That is the colonel through and through. Careless and slipshod." Then he shouted to the driver: "Pull the truck around. I want to get them from the front."

There was no answer from the cab. Without waiting for the order, Gad Ullman leaped onto the steps of the vehicle and swung the door open to get inside. A man standing at the nearest entrance fired at him, the bullets hitting the door. Gad returned the fire instinctively from the hip without even trying to aim. Almost at the same movement he levered himself into the passenger seat and saw the driver lying forward, his head at rest on the steering wheel.

Gad shook the man's shoulder. "For God's sake, turn the truck. We've got to get out of there." The driver's head lolled forward. Ullman grabbed the man's hair and lifted upward so he could see his face. A small black stain stood out in the center of the driver's forehead. A tiny trickle of blood ran down his cheek and over his lips. The eyes were wide open.

Gad did not need more than a second to know that the man was dead. He had been dealing with death too long to require a doctor's opinion on the subject. He pulled the body toward him so that it lay half in the passenger seat and half on the floor of the cab. He slid behind the wheel, and at the second attempt the engine roared into life. He turned the steering wheel slowly to the left. As the right tire of the truck mounted the pavement, the far end of the driver's cab almost scraped the wall of the building. The truck moved with agonizing slowness.

With his left hand Mike grasped the bars that protected the vertical exhaust pipe of the vehicle. In his other hand he held his machine gun. He saw the wall of the old house rearing up in front of him, and in the same instant he also made out the black rectangular entrance at the front of the house, directly opposite the garage doors. The angle between the driver's cab of the truck and its trailer widened slowly.

Suddenly Mike was above the figure that stood just inside one pillar of the entrance. Only a few inches separated the two men. Mike stood over him, on the iron step of the truck. He had anticipated finding a man there. He knew what to expect. Even in the total darkness of the doorway the Mossad commander could see the whites of the man's eyes. He had a look of total surprise.

Then Mike saw the machine gun in the man's hand. They stared at each other for a moment, eye to eye, man to man. Mike's gun was pointing downward, straight into the face of his opponent. The man's reactions were tremendously fast; he began firing with the automatic reflexes of a born fighter. Bullets sprayed the lower part of the truck cabin, a few inches from where Mike was standing.

Now it was the Mossad commander's turn. The burst of fire lit up his assailant's eyes. Within a matter of seconds his face disintegrated into a pulp of dark liquid and shattered bone, and he fell backward, a terrible scream issuing

137

from what had once been a mouth. Then there was silence.

The engine of the truck revved up as Gad carefully accelerated. The entire right side of the vehicle rose onto the paving stones now and moved parallel to a wall. From another entrance to the same building, a man leaped out several yards in front of the truck. The slim weapon in his hands spat out glowing bullets which smashed into the truck's windshield.

Gad Ullman had spotted him in the nick of time. He pushed hard against the door of the cab which was still open. Gripping the wheel with one hand, he leaned out as far as he could, without taking his foot off the accelerator. The assailant's bullets turned the metal wall at the rear of the driver's seat into a sieve. As the man retreated, Gad Ullman went after him as though driving a tank.

He accelerated, gripping the window frame of the open door with his left hand and keeping his head down and as far to the left as he could to avoid getting hit. The retreating figure was framed between the driver's door and the windshield frame.

The headlights of Gad's vehicle flooded the street, illuminating it like the stage of a theater. Now he could identify the weapon in the man's hand. A Kalashnikov. The truck's lights, coming straight for him, dazzled the man. He fired wildly where he thought the invisible driver must be seated.

As he blazed away at the head of the advancing foe, the truck came roaring nearer and nearer. Too late he tried to lower his weapon to shoot out the brilliant lights focused on him. Running backward toward the wall, he tried to squeeze himself into the entrance from which he had emerged, in an attempt to find sanctuary from the unstoppable monster coming straight at him.

He realized he was not going to make it. The truck was closer than he was to the entrance. Again he fired. This time the silent bullets found their target. They ripped into the left headlight of the truck, shattering it. Still the vehicle came at him. It was now actually scraping against jutting sections of the building wall.

He made one more attempt to all but force himself into

the stonework of the wall. Again he pulled the trigger, but only a single bullet was fired. The firing-pin struck an empty breech; there was no more ammunition.

In fury, the man flung his gun at the approaching truck, then turned to run. But panic-stricken now, he turned too sharply and lost his footing. He threw his arm up and forward to break his fall against the paving. As he half rose, he was sent sprawling by a violent blow to his back. It was the fender of the truck.

He tried to escape by rolling into the center of the pavement, aiming to get between the wheels of the advancing vehicle. Then something struck his head. There was a noise of crunching bone as the heavy truck ground first his foot, then his knees, and finally the rest of his body between its wheels and the hard paving stones. There was one shrill shriek, then silence. The truck continued for twenty yards down the center of the street after swinging off the pavement, then came to a halt.

When it was over, Mike's men counted six bodies and quickly dragged them into the garage. "We'll deal with them later," he said. He ordered Ruby to check the damage to the truck. "We won't be able to show up at the dock gate with something that looks more like a sieve than a transport vehicle," he said.

Ruby examined the truck carefully. The engine cover and the doors were full of holes. The windshield was shattered, as was the left headlight. Mike shook his head. He was worried. Ruby seemed undismayed, however. "Don't worry," he said. "We can cover up those holes with ordinary Elastoplast. They won't notice them at this time of night." He pointed to the windshield. "We'll have to take out the rest of the glass. Its absence won't be spotted in the dark either."

The headlight was a problem though. Ruby examined it closely. Then, taking tools from the pocket of his blue coverall which he had hardly taken off during the past days in the garage, he got to work, helped by another agent. Ten minutes later, the truck was ready to go. It was a little the worse for wear, but there was no damage to its engine or to the container. The quick, external touch-ups would not stand close scrutiny, but Mike felt that they were good enough to get by.

Once again, Ruby Goldman had saved them. When Mike congratulated him, the mechanic simply smiled and said quietly: "I had to find a way. We have no choice in the matter." It was as simple as that.

As they pulled out of the street, there were almost no signs of the battle that had raged there only a short time before. Some shattered glass lay in the gutters and on the pavement, there were bloodstains, and the nearby walls and doors were pockmarked with bullet holes, but none of it showed in the dark. And when daylight broke, the team would be far away.

The body of the slain Mossad driver was hidden in the garage. His death had necessitated a change of plan. Mike drove his car behind the truck until they were close to the docks. Then he parked and climbed into the driver's seat, taking over from Gad.

They drove through the checkpoint without difficulty. It was misty and cold, a typical November evening. The guard did not waste any time with the documents thrust in front of him. He glanced at them with a quick, practiced eye, and without bothering to turn his flashlight in the direction of the truck, he waved them through, then hurried out of the winter's damp back to the comfort of his heated and well-lit guardhouse.

Chapter Sixteen

The truck, now covered with stained pieces of Elastoplast and without a windshield, moved slowly between the rows of sheds in the port of Antwerp. Only one vessel had her working lights on and was in the process of loading cargo: the *Scheersberg A*. Squat-looking barrels marked with the innocuous word "plumbat" in white letters were gradually filling up her bowels.

The truck seemed in no hurry to reach its destination. Now it moved with only its parking lights to signal its progress. In the shed the daytime bustle was gone. There was very little activity, and only a few men were about.

The vehicle with the container standing firm and solid behind the cab came to a gentle stop twenty yards from the shed. Its front faced the entrance.

While the uranium was being lowered into hold Number One, containers which had been stored in the shed were going into hold Number Two. The containers were identical to the one sitting on the back of the truck. They were red, with words stenciled in white paint on their sides. Three more were waiting their turn to be taken out to the *Scheersberg*.

"Just in time!" Mike said tersely.

The fork-lift driver drove up to them. His heavy and powerful machine had impressive weights attached at the back and made a loud racket. It moved quite slowly, but then it was not built for speed. Its virtue was in its enormous lifting power and steadiness under massive weights of cargo.

The two men in the driver's cabin watched the fork-lift driver approach with apprehension. No one had anticipated that curiosity would cause any dock employee to go out of his way to see what the truck was up to. The fork-lift driver looked at the two shadowy figures in the vehicle and then with surprise at the container which it had just brought to the shed. He glanced down at a clipboard in front of him and a puzzled look crossed his face. The extra container did not tally with the number of trips he had to make, according to his work sheet for the shift.

Still he did not stop; he passed the truck and made a short detour to enter the shed. Mike and his companion watched tensely. What was he going to do? Would he telephone the security office to check?

The driver stopped his fork-lift near one of the three remaining red containers that *were* supposed to be loaded into the *Scheersberg*. He began to maneuver methodically in order to raise it aloft.

Mike turned to watch the casual progress of another dock-yard worker who was wandering among the crates and cases. He approached the fork-lift driver, who was deeply engrossed in his labors, without being noticed. The only other personnel around were on the far side of the shed. They were busy with a tidying operation, moving cases of cargo to be ready for loading in the morning.

The steel bar struck the fork-lift driver in the back of the neck at the precise moment that the metal prongs of the machine were thrust deep beneath the container. The man fell forward. The blow had been delivered with scientific exactitude; he was not dead, but he would be unconscious for quite some time. As he pitched forward, the strong arms of his assailant grabbed him around the chest and gently eased him to the ground.

Mike was out of his seat like a flash of lightning. Seconds later he was helping the wielder of the steel bar drag the fork-lift driver behind some crates, where more of the useful roll of Elastoplast was stuck over his mouth. His hands were tied, and then his feet. Still unconscious, he was dumped behind boxes of cargo and covered with a few empty cardboard cartons that were lying around.

The fork-lift now had a new operator. The driver of the Mossad truck was back in his seat. The container moved backward on the steel prongs as the operator reversed the machine. He raised the container and drove out of the shed.

No one had seen the incident, nor did anyone notice that instead of heading for the ship, the fork-lift operator moved the container to the dark side of the shed where, as had been carefully noted in advance by the artist-agent, some lights were missing. The container was temporarily dumped there.

The fork-lift then approached the waiting trailer truck and swiftly lifted the container from it. Ten minutes later the container was being stowed neatly into the hold of the *Scheersberg* to join the other similarly colored holders of cargo. Two hours later the loading of the ship was complete.

The stamped papers that the truck driver handed over as his vehicle left the dock yards aroused no suspicion. The guard realized immediately that the truck was carrying the same red container with which it had arrived. After the fork-lift machine had lowered the "Trojan horse" container into the hold of the waiting ship, Mike's men had replaced it with the one that they had left standing outside in the dark shadows of the shed.

"Can't make up their bloody minds," the driver grumbled to the security man. "First they tell me to bring it tonight on special delivery, and then I have to take it out again."

The port official nodded his head sympathetically, as if to say: "That's the way it is with bureaucracy." Then he added cheerfully: "Never mind. I'm sure you're being paid overtime. So you should worry!"

As soon as they were out of sight of the port entrance, Mike got out of the truck. His voice was harsh and angry as he told the driver to go back to the garage and "help clean up the mess."

"I have some business to attend to," he added with cold

143

menace. "Then I'll be back to give you a hand." His tone was such that his companion did not even dare ask what he had in mind; he did precisely what he was told, and drove off. The shiver that ran up his spine had nothing to do with the lack of a windshield on a cold night. He knew Mike well enough to realize that his boss was in his most ruthless and deadly mood, and he was very glad indeed that the "business" had nothing to do with him.

It was noon on the 17th of November, some six and a half hours after the *Scheersberg A*, its Liberian flag drooping lifelessly from the mast in the damp, misty dawn, had made its way out of Antwerp harbor and put out to sea. At that very moment, Officer Willhelm Smitt of the Brussels police force decided to take a closer look at the black Mercedes with diplomatic license plates parked in Rembrandt Street. He had spotted the man sleeping at the wheel earlier, and had passed the same vehicle three times since then. Theoretically he should have handed out a parking ticket, but he knew it was a pointless exercise. The fine would never be paid. Foreign diplomats did just as they liked and took no notice of any summons involving minor traffic offenses.

Finally, he decided that action had to be taken. The man was still sleeping at the wheel in precisely the same position as when Smitt had first spotted him. The police officer approached the car cautiously and tapped lightly on the windshield. There was no response.

It was then that the officer noticed the strange angle of the man's head, as well as the blue-gray color of his lips. He opened the door quickly and carefully prodded the man's arm. Then, as he tapped him on the shoulder, the body spilled out of the open door onto the road like a sack of potatoes.

At the pathology department of the Brussels police force, the doctor on duty summed up the results of his careful examination of the corpse in a one-page report. *"Death due to fracture of the spinal cord in the neck."* There were further technical details, all of which clearly indicated that a violent blow of the fist or some other instrument had brought the life of the victim to an abrupt end.

It was not until that evening that the identity of the victim was discovered. He was Colonel Habib Boudija, the assistant attaché for cultural affairs at the Moroccan embassy in Paris.

The senior diplomat who came to police headquarters by train from the French capital the following morning did not seem very grieved by the death of his colleague. In fact, he did his utmost to hush up the affair; every lever he could pull was employed to "avoid a fuss."

Mike was now back in Antwerp. Although he was very worried, the look of suppressed fury in his eyes was no longer there. The Moroccan colonel had sold him down the river, but it was an action he would never be able to repeat. In the meantime, Mike had a lot of bodies on his hands and one tremendous problem. How far had Boudija's treachery gone?

The identity of the dead attackers stacked in the grease pit of the garage shed a little light on the subject. Some of them were known Egyptian "strong-arm" men who worked out of Rome. One of them had been involved in the kidnapping of an Israeli traitor named Mordechai Louk, who had deserted to the Egyptians and had become a spy for them. When he tried to double-cross his new masters he was kidnapped in broad daylight in Rome, drugged, and placed in a box to be shipped by plane to Cairo. The plot misfired when the aircraft was delayed; Louk woke prematurely and started shouting. Hearing his cries, Italian customs men freed him from the box. The Egyptians who carried out the seizure of Louk had escaped at the time, but now one of them lay dead in an Antwerp garage.

The Mossad commander had to think fast. It was clear that the colonel had sold the information about the nuclear fuel to the Egyptians. Perhaps he had even sold them the uranium. That was it! The colonel *had* sold the Egyptians the uranium!

Going over the chain of events, Mike realized now what Boudija had been up to. The purpose of the attack on the garage had not been simply to kill him and his squad. If this had been the intent, the Egyptians could have chosen the noisier but safer and far simpler method of planting a bomb. They had tried to kill his men silently in order to gain control of the container. Had they succeeded, four Egyptians would now be in the hold of the *Scheersberg A*, instead of his Mossad team. They would have seized the vessel and headed for Alexandria.

"The cunning bastard," Mike mused. "How many other customers had he sold the shipment of uranium to? Just how many people had he double-crossed?" It was all fitting together like a jigsaw puzzle. Suddenly, the colonel's suggestion that he hand over the photographs of the two crewmen who were to arrive in Marseilles hit Mike like a blow between the eyes.

The colonel must have told the Egyptians that Mike was going to send two of his men aboard the vessel disguised as Moroccans. His spies, still on the Antwerp docks, had reported that two more men *had* joined the *Scheersberg A*, but security was so tight that they could not be sure that the pair were Meir Azoulai and Shauli Mizrachi.

It was quite possible that his two operators in Marseilles had been intercepted. In that case, how much had the Egyptians extracted from his two "Moroccan seamen"? He knew that they were among the best agents he had ever commanded. Even so, despite the harsh training they had undergone, there was never any guarantee that in the end they could not be broken. The two men might have been tortured. They might even be dead.

Possibly they had talked. Possibly they had given the Egyptians and the colonel information about the container and the garage in Antwerp. It could be that this was how they had so nearly been ambushed the night before. In that case, who were the two men who had boarded the *Scheersberg*? They could be Egyptian or Moroccan agents, or any other agents for that matter. It depended on whom the colonel had sold the uranium to, in his chain of greedy betrayal.

Mike was in a desperate situation. His men were waiting in a container. They could wait in vain for their two colleagues to free them. On the other hand, it was quite possible that the two men on board were going to try and kill his "pirates." Yet he could not be sure of this. Since all the attackers at the garage had been killed, there was no way of persuading any of them to tell him what the

Egyptians really knew. How could they have discovered about the container? Mike had never told Boudija about it.

How could he warn his men? They were deep in the hold of the uranium ship, sealed into the container. There was no way in which he could contact them. No way to tell them that they were not going to be released as planned. And if they *were* released . . .

All four men were first-rate professionals. Under any other circumstances Mike was confident that they could get themselves out of any unexpected trouble. That was what all the rigorous training in the Special Operations Division was about. But now they were locked up in a dark hold, with no freedom of action. They had no option but to wait, passive victims of circumstance. He knew that if they were found they would be killed, or at the very best handed over to the Italian, Moroccan, or Egyptian authorities.

In either event there was only one outcome to the mission: total failure. The valuable cargo would not reach its destination—Dimona. He would be back at square one.

That night, Mike made contact with the commander of the Israeli navy from the embassy in Brussels. He asked him to prepare his men for Plan Two. This was an emergency operation which everyone had hoped would not be necessary. None of them really wanted to risk it unless there was no alternative. Now it seemed they had no choice.

According to Plan Two, Israeli ships would ambush the *Scheersberg A* at a predetermined spot on the high seas. The barrels would be unloaded at gunpoint. It would be a clear-cut case of piracy. But instead of robbing the stricken vessel of pieces-of-eight, as did the pirates of old in the Mediterranean, there were now much higher stakes. If Mike's guess was right, the sea ambush would have to take place at a point about one day's sailing from the Egyptian port of Alexandria.

"That is," he thought to himself, "if it *is* the Egyptians who are going to get it, and if the Moroccan colonel did not sell it to somebody else a few hours before he met his sudden end."

Chapter Seventeen

In the Number Two hold of the *Scheersberg A*, four men sat tense and silent. They hardly dared breathe. The sound of cautious footsteps was heard above their heads. Two men, wearing soft-soled shoes, were exploring the hold. Obviously the pair were looking for them, but something was very wrong. According to the plan, which they all knew by heart, the two were supposed to release them from the container on the *second* night of sailing. For some reason, they were going to be released a mere eighteen hours after leaving Antwerp—on the first night.

Why?

With the true instincts of the primitive hunter who lives or dies by his cunning and guile, or lack of it, Gad Ullman took hold of his Beretta .22 and attached the silencer to it. The others looked at their luminous watches. It was ten minutes after midnight. It was now the 18th of November. Not only was the day wrong, but the two Mossad agents aboard the ship were to have come for them at 2:00 A.M. Perhaps their colleagues had received orders changing the timetable before they boarded the ship.

They switched on the small lamp connected to the battery they had brought along just for this purpose. It could not be seen through the metal walls of the container. They listened to the voices of the two men who were now standing directly above them. There was no mistake about it. It was their colleagues looking for them.

Ruby Goldman picked up a welding hammer. He raised it to knock on the metal wall of the container with the prearranged code signal that meant all was well. Just as he was about to strike, Gad Ullman's arm snaked out and his fingers closed on Ruby's wrist with the strength of a steel vise. The two were so close that the mechanic could feel the "Exterminator's" breath hot on his cheek. Ruby froze, hardly daring to let out the air in his lungs. Obviously something was desperately wrong. Otherwise Gad Ullman would not be nearly breaking his wrist to restrain him.

The footsteps passed over the roof of the container. There was no mistaking the reason for Ullman's action now. The two men were speaking in Arabic. Softly, it was true, softly enough so that it was impossible to hear their precise words, but it was Arabic all right. No mistake about that. The faint lamp was extinguished—just in case.

The four men sat like pillars of rock. The voices above them were a little louder now. Their frustration showed through. They seemed unable to find what they were looking for. All the containers were the same size; all bore the same markings. Unless they knew where to find the secret marking, there was no way of telling which one was serving as the home for the four Mossad agents.

The Arabs were tapping on each container in turn with some metallic object. If they had had any doubts before, all four now knew these were *not* their two companions. There was to be no tapping. The signal was to be made in an entirely different way. If the knocking was intended to trap them, then it was a ploy that was most certainly not going to work. For two and a half hours the two men searched and re-searched the hold. Then they left.

To the four men in the container the situation was crystal clear. The plan had gone wrong. Their two colleagues had been replaced by two hostile strangers. They had no idea who they represented, but they were Arabs; it hardly mattered which Arabs. One thing was certain: their intent was not friendly.

The Mossad agents knew their situation verged on the

desperate. They could count on no help from the outside. They were sealed in an enormous steel coffin, which was, in turn, hemmed in on both sides, on top and below by a number of other containers. It was true that there were release handles on two sides of their "home," but these could only be manipulated from the outside.

Just as Mike had figured it out, the purpose of the garage attack now became clear to the four men. The intent had been to kill them, but, more important, to place someone else—Arabs—in the container and then hijack the ship for their own purposes. They had been aware, as was the Mossad commander, that some of the attackers had been Egyptians.

Suddenly a gleam of hope surged up in Gad Ullman. "Listen," he said softly. "The two men on the ship. How do they know that the attack on the garage failed? Nobody got away. We are certain of that. Or just about certain. In any event, it would have been too late to warn the men on the ship since they must have climbed aboard earlier in the day. So they *must* believe that they are looking for their friends. They weren't being careless calling out in Arabic. They just don't realize that it is not fellow-Arabs they are looking for! So we still have the element of surprise in our favor!"

It was like an intricate dance—error heaped upon error, just as the containers were heaped one on another. Different sets of agents were being misled by the rapid turn of events. One thing, however, was certain. The two men would return to seek out their comrades. And there was no doubt about another fact. The takeover of the ship, which originally should have taken place without any casualties, was going to involve a fight. There were going to be dead men. Either two dead Arabs or four dead Israelis.

It was daytime now. The two men would not be coming below. To do so would simply warn the rest of the crew of their intentions. The men in the container switched on the small light and turned instinctively toward Ruby. For a minute three pairs of eyes were riveted on him. He did not even seem to notice his companions. Then suddenly he got up and went over to the miniature welding and cutting machine that had been stowed away in the container for quite a different purpose.

Working fast, but carefully, he adjusted the bottle of compressed oxygen and set the pressure gauge. Turning the oxyacetylene machine down as low as he could and tapping the steel walls of the container with a small hammer, he finally decided to cut the escape hatch on the narrow west side of their home.

He brought the machine over carefully and set it right against the wall. They all realized this was the only way of getting out of the container without alerting the ship's crew. Ruby did not like to spell it out, but he knew that the operation was so dangerous that it bordered on madness.

From their position sealed in the container, they did not have the faintest idea of where in the ship's hold their home, which was beginning to look more and more like a premature coffin, was situated. Consequently they did not have the faintest idea of what lay on the other side of the section they were going to cut through. If it was made of wood or some other inflammable material, the flame of the cutter piercing the metal would turn it into an instant inferno. The blaze would spread throughout the hold long before any attempt could be made to bring it under control. There was no chance that the ship—or they—could survive. And even if the container beside them was made of metal, it was quite possible that its contents were such that the heat could set it on fire.

Ruby kept his thoughts to himself. With the help of his companions he removed all the equipment stored near the area where he was going to cut. He gripped the cutting apparatus with a steady hand, focused the flame on the center of the wall, and got to work. It was a very slow and painstaking job. Ruby had to be careful not to turn the full blast of the flame against the wall. He had to try and calculate with infinite precision the exact moment that he penetrated the wall of his own container, so that the flame would not burst through with a savage jet of heat. Only the very tip of the flame must stab into the darkness beyond.

The thin, vertical cut was made with agonizing slowness. When it reached a length of twenty-five inches,

Ruby made a right angle so that he was now cutting horizontally. Slowly, fraction of an inch by fraction of an inch, the flame crawled along the steel wall. He cut for some two feet, then downward vertically again. The three men watched him as though hypnotized. He was like a machine himself. He *was* the machine. The incision was made as though it had been guided by carefully drawn lines, invisible to anyone other than Ruby. His arm never seemed to waver. It was uncanny the way he worked.

Finally at 6:30 on the evening of the 18th, a rectangular piece of metal, carefully supported by pliers just before the final breakthrough, was deposited on the floor of the container. All four men climbed out. Now they could see that their container had been loaded on the top row, against the wall of the ship. It was possible to walk, crouching, across their own roof, just beneath the steel hatches of the hold. The entire upper part of the hold was filled with containers, one next to the other.

The four men moved noiselessly over the containers. They spread out through the hold. Gad Ullman took up a position between two containers on the left side of the ship. In this spot, hidden up to his head, he could cover the entrance to the hold and the small stepladder next to it. It was a mere ten yards away. He was certain that if the two Arabs went below to seek their companions, this is where they would enter the hold. It was the entrance on the cargo deck directly under the bridge.

To see this point, the man on watch on the bridge would have to stick his head out of the glass window in front of him; to get a proper view of the entrance he would be forced to lean the whole upper half of his body out. On that cold November night, in the middle of the Bay of Biscay, it was highly doubtful that any sane officer, no matter how dutiful, would perform such a maneuver. In any event, why should he bother with such vigilance? No crew member could possibly want to go down into the cargo hold.

There was another opening to the hold, toward the front. It faced the bulkhead between Hold One and Hold Two. However, this opening was clearly visible from the bridge, and since it was also entirely blocked by a container, it was evident to the four men that the "visitors" really had only one way of descending into the target area.

Gad Ullman checked his .22 Beretta once again. He tightened the silencer on the barrel and tried the cocking mechanism. Then he put it down on the roof of the container in front of him. All he had to do was wait.

Ze'ev Biran and Ruby Goldman had taken up strategic firing positions in the center of the hold, well concealed between the containers. The Berettas in their hands were also fitted with silencers. Although both men were crack shots, they knew that they were no match for Gad Ullman. They would leave the shooting to him, intervening only if something went wrong.

Benny Arnheim stood hidden in the opposite corner of the hold. He was armed with a Beretta, and he too knew how to use it, as did every man in the Mossad, regardless of his specialty.

They waited for almost four hours. At 10:25 all four were alerted by the sound of scraping above them. The trapdoor over the entrance was raised slowly and evenly. The light of the moon illuminated the narrow entrance through which the steps of the ladder passed into the hold. A pair of feet in what looked like light, rubber-soled tennis shoes were cautiously poised on the top rung of the ladder.

The pair of feet lowered themselves step by step very slowly until their owner materialized and stepped across lightly onto the top of the nearest container right next to the ladder. He tapped on the ladder with the unlit flashlight he was holding to signal to his companion to follow him. The second man was heavier in movement than the first. He came down the ladder, outlined square in the light which penetrated through the opening of the hold. His friend approached him. The second man stood on the bottom rung of the ladder, his body leaning against it to balance himself. With both hands he slowly began to lower the heavy steel cover.

Two dull thuds followed each other. They were so close to one another that the second shot seemed like an echo of the first. The cover crashed down with a heavy metallic thud. The two men fell in a heap onto a container.

The only sound in the hold was a slight rustling noise. It was caused by the second man, who had been standing on the ladder, only a second or two before. His leg was shaking in a strange, convulsive way and scraping against the metal top of the container. The leg contracted and straightened out in a series of rapid movements, then lay motionless.

Gad Ullman was the first to act. He moved to check the results of his handiwork.

With the thin beam of his flashlight he peered into the faces of the two men he had shot. In his other hand he held the Beretta—just in case. Neither of the pair was any longer in the land of the living. He had done it with two shots. Two victims. His one-hundred-percent record was still intact.

On the bridge of the *Scheersberg*, Captain Peter Barrow emerged from the lighted chart room and stepped into the darkness. He was absolutely sure that he had heard a dull thud or a similar noise coming from the direction of the deck below. He asked the sailor on watch if he had heard anything. The man, an old salt, nodded his head. He had heard a sound "like falling metal." He did not admit it, but the noise had awakened him from his dozing. He had been at sea all his life and had spent more hours on long night watches than he cared to remember. Over the years, he had perfected the technique of drowsing while standing up. He could lean against the windshield on the wing of the bridge without the duty officer detecting what he was doing.

Captain Peter Barrow listened very carefully now. His eyes were still trying to adjust to the darkness after the light of the chart room. He lit the beam that was fixed to the corner of the bridge. Its powerful rays bathed the deck with sudden brilliance. Both he and the sailor swept the area with their eyes. There was nothing to be seen. Everything was in order. The lamp was extinguished, and the captain went back to his work in the chart room.

In Hold Two of the *Scheersberg A* the four Mossad men completed their last preparations. The bodies of the two dead Egyptians were dragged to the rear wall of the hold. At 4:40 A.M. the deck was still blanketed in winter's darkness. Four figures slipped one after the other through the square opening in front of the superstructure. They turned into the external passageway between the ship's rail and the bridge area, and continued along it until they reached the stern of the vessel. Then they turned once more. Now they began to climb slowly up the wooden stairway behind the bridge.

The first officer, Barney MacDowell, stood with his legs apart by the right-hand rail of the bridge, behind the azimuth measure. In his right hand he held his sextant, in his left a stopwatch. He was waiting until the horizon became clear. It was still too dark and misty for him to measure the angle of elevation of any star.

He liked the dawn hours, "the time of star-hunting" as he called it. His task was to measure the angle of elevation and the times of the navigational stars, one after the other, before they were swallowed up in the brightening sky. He had to work fast in order to catch as many of them as possible in the shortest period of time. When visibility conditions permitted, he could measure seven or more stars with the sextant. He would work out the angles of the hour of the "true altitude" and the "true azimuth" from the navigational tables. This enabled him to determine the "position line." Then he would draw them on a chart. It was a fairly straightforward mechanical operation, but it did have one advantage: it helped pass a considerable part of the morning watch hours.

Barney leaned over the azimuth measure and pointed it toward Venus. As he did, from the corner of his eye he saw a man standing right next to him. For an instant he thought it was the sailor on the watch who wanted something. He turned, slightly irritated at the interruption. The barrel of a Beretta with a silencer attached pointed straight at his chest.

Like a trapped animal looking for rescue, Barney MacDowell shot a glance to the other side of the bridge where the sailor of the watch was standing. He was staring out to sea and had not noticed the man with the gun. The two doors of the wheel house were open. Barney could pick out a figure bent over the bridge rail. But he had no idea of what was happening on the rest of the bridge.

The stranger with the revolver in his hand was standing a little way from him now, so that the sailor would not see him. Barney felt a shiver of fear spread throughout his body. He held his breath and shut his eyes. For one desperate moment a wave of hysteria swept him and he wanted to scream out. However, no sound could pass the tight band of terror now gripping the muscles of his throat.

In excellent English, the man with the gun said: "Just take it easy. I am not going to shoot you. Now listen carefully. Don't shout. Don't move. From this moment, I am the commander of this ship. I regret giving you a fright. I suggest you cooperate fully. Simply carry on with your duties as though nothing has happened. But please, don't try and be a hero. If you attempt anything not ordered by me, I want you to know this gun is not a toy. And I will not hesitate for a second to use it."

The stranger had caught the first officer's glance toward the sailor on the other side of the bridge.

"Call him over, please. You can ask him to get you a cup of tea. But no unnecessary remarks. For your sake."

Barney MacDowell called the man over. His voice sounded like the far-off croak of a frog. His mouth was so still and dry he could hardly say another word. Lifting his left hand, the stopwatch still clutched in it, up to his mouth, he made a silent signal which was immediately understood: he wanted something to drink.

The sailor had still not spotted the man with the gun. Quite deliberately, the stranger had stood behind the steel bulkhead of the bridge, shielding himself from view.

"Please go into the wheel house," said the gunman as soon as the sailor had gone down from the bridge to get the tea. The first officer did as he was told.

"Put down your navigation instruments. Now waken the captain on the internal telephone and call him to the bridge. Don't explain why."

Captain Peter Barrow was not very pleased at being gotten out of his bed at such an early hour. "Can't you manage without me," he grumbled sleepily.

The anxious tones of his first officer told him otherwise. "Please come to the bridge immediately."

Now wide awake, he leaped out of bed. Seconds later, wrapped in his red toweling bathrobe, he came rushing into the chart room. In a single glance he immediately understood the reason his first officer had sounded tense and frightened. There was not just one man with a gun now. Standing in the entrance of the chart room was another stranger, a gray-haired man who was also armed.

It was this second uninvited visitor who spoke: "From this moment on, I am in charge of the ship." He smiled reassuringly. "Please don't worry. And don't be frightened. We bear you no ill-will whatsoever. You are perfectly safe—as long as you obey orders. Your ship will come to no harm. I have captain's papers and a considerable amount of sea-going experience. All you have to do is listen to me carefully and obey.

"You will be worried about what the owners have to say. They will not be angry with you. Your owners are, in fact, no longer your owners, if you understand what I mean. You will receive radio notification of this some time today. To make everything agreeable for all of us, let's work together."

It was only at this moment that the skipper caught sight of yet another stranger bending over the instrument panel in the small wireless room of the *Scheersberg*. This room was normally separated from the chart room by a dingy curtain, but at this moment it was half open.

Following the captain's gaze, the man with the gray hair said: "Forgive me if I seem suspicious. I really am sorry about this, but the radio is being adjusted at this minute. From now on, you can only receive messages. You cannot transmit."

A few hours after the four Mossad men left their container and took over the *Scheersberg A*, the first hint that disaster had hit the uranium project began to leak through to Morocco. General Muhammed Ofkir was wild with anger when he finally pieced together the series of events stemming from the efforts of his agent in Paris to double-cross everyone in sight. Because the general was a man who never forgot his honor as a former French-trained officer, he promptly gave back every ounce of gold to the Indians, even the percentage they had given him as a sweetener.

What stung him particularly were the angry reactions of both the Egyptians and the Israelis. Colonel Habib Boudija's double-cross reflected on Ofkir's own standing and reputation throughout the intelligence community of the Arab world, in Tel Aviv, and in Western countries including the United States. News of the incident spread quickly, as did details of Boudija's violent end. A man of extreme sensitivity where his reputation was concerned, the general was slow to cool down.

Within weeks, the details of the uranium operation were known in every capital in the West. It was decided by mutual agreement to keep the matter a secret—and so it remained for nine years until Paul Leventhal, representing the United States at an antinuclear conference in Europe, revealed the disappearance of the *Scheersberg*'s cargo.

Chapter Eighteen

At noon on the 19th of November, just as the four "hijackers" of the *Scheersberg* had promised, the owners of the vessel made radio contact. Briefly they informed Captain Peter Barrow of the change. However his instructions were clear: "Continue to Genoa as originally planned." It was the last contact that the owners made with the vessel.

Benny Arnheim radioed his reply that the message had been received. Then, for the second time, he disconnected the broadcasting mechanism and the automatic distress device.

The four men who had suddenly emerged from the hold of the vessel treated Captain Peter Barrow and his first officer, Barney MacDowell, politely and correctly. Both men tried to make the best of the situation; they had little choice since they were unarmed. Barrow, remembering the peculiar noise during the previous night, put two and two together and guessed what had happened: that the four had somehow hidden themselves in one of the containers brought aboard at Antwerp. He did not ask any questions, for he realized that he was not going to get any answers.

He knew that the men had no interest in his vessel; they were after the cargo of uranium. He was well aware of its value, having taken the trouble to make inquiries and do some private research before sailing. The four new men came as a surprise to the crew. There was much speculation about their sudden appearance and also about the disappearance of two of their colleagues. But no one asked their opinion, and they simply went on with their work.

Life aboard ship continued normally as the *Scheersberg* headed out into the Atlantic, rounding the Iberian Peninsula before passing through the Straits of Gibraltar. From the crew's point of view the only thing that seemed at all unusual was that the four men made use of the captain's cabin as though it was their own. One of them was always seated inside it. Unseen, however, was the way he kept watch over a stock of weapons and some mysterious boxes and other equipment that had been brought out of the hold. The British captain and his first officer continued their normal routine of keeping watch on the bridge, but always in the company of one of the four men.

Everything was going according to plan.

The phone at Mike's bedside rang. It was Sharon, her voice tense: "The rival paper has scooped me. They've discovered that I have some pictures that don't belong to me. And they are going to try and get them back!"

Something had gone wrong. What Sharon was telling him was that Euratom was now aware that the uranium cargo was in the hands of unauthorized individuals. It might well be that the European governments had been clued in too.

When the short message to the *Scheersberg* had brought the answer he had prayed for, the Mossad commander had thought his troubles were over. He knew his men would not let him down. They had obviously realized that the two crew members who had been planted aboard were not genuine. Evidently they had managed to get out of the container and had overpowered the two Arab agents and seized the ship as planned.

Mike could only guess about the leak to Euratom. Perhaps General Muhammed Ofkir had discovered that his colonel was dead and put two and two together. By passing on the message to Euratom about the hijack of the cargo he might have thought he would be able to salvage something.

More likely, the Mossad commander reasoned, it was Bikbashi Fuad Abdul Nasser who had decided to let the cat out of the bag. The Egyptian secret service man might have wanted revenge for the disappearance of six of his best men. This was one eventuality that Mike had not anticipated. It hadn't occurred to him that the authorities might hear about the plan to spirit away two hundred tons of uranium which were never supposed to leave the jurisdiction of the Common Market.

The affair was known. That was evident. The last part of the operation was most certainly *not* going to be smooth sailing.

It was Antonio Bordini who had sounded the warning. He had called Sharon Manners as soon as he got wind of the "leak." One of the security officers at Euratom, in a state of great agitation, had said that an "almighty investigation" was going on inside the organization at that very moment.

The unconscious fork-lift operator had been found in Antwerp. The Belgian authorities were puzzled by the incident. Nothing had been stolen. The man was still too dazed to explain how he had come to be tied up behind a pile of crates in a shed on the docks. But since he *had* been loading uranium when the assault had occurred, Euratom was alerted immediately.

Euratom's security arrangements were not all that they might have been. Even now, in a state of emergency, there was a considerable amount of bureaucratic delay. Antonio Bordini dragged his feet about supplying information concerning the deals that had been negotiated, all quite legal and aboveboard, in connection with the uranium then sailing in the hold of the *Scheersberg*.

The Société Générale des Minerais, Asmara's purchasing agent, Herbert Schulzen, as well as the Italian firm of SAICA were all contacted. The Milan firm confirmed the report: "Yes, we are expecting a shipment to reach us via Genoa." They had, in fact, received $12,000 "in advance to process it."

Mike knew that the Euratom officials were not fools. It would eventually dawn on someone at headquarters that the answer to the questions being asked could only be provided by locating the *Scheersberg*. For all he knew, the search was already on. Certainly the governments of the Common Market would be alerted. At this very moment their planes and naval vessels could be scouring the Mediterranean for the ship. The CIA might be dragged in, and that meant that the American Sixth Fleet would also be on the lookout for the "uranium ship."

The whole operation now hung on a slender thread. Every minute that passed increased the chances of the *Scheersberg* being seized at sea and taken into custody, to be brought back to Antwerp.

The Mossad commander hurried to the Israeli embassy building in Paris. Abandoning all precautions, he did not wait for the prearranged time to communicate with his men. According to plan, he made brief contact each day at precisely 7:30 to ensure that all was going well.

He glanced quickly at his watch. It was 6:30. The 27th of November.

Mike's guesswork had been accurate.

As he was hurrying to the embassy building, several planes of the NATO command had already been given precise orders: "Find the *Scheersberg*."

The air force command had been told that the command came from above and that it had to be carried out immediately. At 5:45 precisely, about half an hour before sunset, a reconnaissance plane flew low over the *Scheersberg*. It buzzed the vessel three times, flying its length. Then it made two additional dives at right angles to the ship before it disappeared heading north.

Captain Ze'ev Biran watched the aircraft anxiously. "The game is beginning to warm up," he said to Gad Ullman, who was standing next to him. "They have been taking photographs of us. And it's not for a beauty contest!"

The commander of the *Scheersberg* did not have long to wait for an answer to his unasked question: What was a NATO plane doing buzzing him?

Mike used the emergency alarm previously worked out

in detail with Benny Arnheim. There was an attachment to the usual frequency that activated a warning signal on the sensitive instrument panel installed by Benny in the ship's radio room. The radio operator hardly ever moved from his seat next to the chart room. When he slept or was forced to go to the toilet, he told one of his three colleagues to take his place and to call him the moment the instrument panel sprang to life.

It was a wearisome business, sitting there hour after hour. The only break in routine came with meals. Even then, Benny sat eating with the tray of food in such a position that the equipment was always under his careful eye.

The coded message that now came over from Paris was signed by Mike. He urgently needed to know the present position of the ship. Sixty seconds later it was relayed to him.

And almost immediately Captain Ze'ev Biran had his answer: *"You have been detected. You must disappear. Proceed with Plan Three."*

That was all. Mike did not elaborate, for he knew that radio operators all along the Mediterranean would be alerted by now. His message was in code, but NATO had computers that could break codes. He was not going to give away anything more than was absolutely necessary.

Captain Ze'ev Biran read the decoded message, then carefully examined the sea charts. Plan Three required an enormous amount of preparatory work. He thanked his lucky stars that they had taken so much trouble working out the details so that they could switch to this alternative successfully if it was found necessary to do so. And it *was* obviously necessary to do so if the mission was to succeed.

It took Ze'ev Biran only a few minutes to find what he was looking for. It was a small island off Greece, about two hours' sailing northeast. The "island" was in reality little more than a great rock that jutted out abruptly from the sea. It had none of the charm associated with many other Greek islands so eagerly sought after by tourists. The rock island was just that—a rock. On its southern side, it had a small cove with a narrow opening.

The place had been chosen deliberately. If they could anchor in the center of the cove, there was a good chance that they might be able to dodge reconnaissance aircraft—for a short time anyway. Certainly no one could see them at night, and in the early morning the vessel might not be noticed for a few hours since the shadow of the rock would obscure any ship anchored there.

This would give Ruby Goldman time to carry out *his* part—part B of Plan Three.

Captain Ze'ev Biran had been totally unenthusiastic when Mike had first spotted this isolated rock. "I depend on you to anchor there," Mike had said. "There is probably no other skipper alive who can do it, but I know you can. That is why you are on this operation."

The subject was considered closed, but Biran had not been all that sure that he could do it. He had studied the place carefully. It was small, rock-strewn, and surrounded by reefs. To anchor a large ship there during daylight under ideal conditions with first-class equipment and a crack crew would be difficult enough.

The trouble was that the *Scheersberg* was ill-equipped. And Biran did not have much confidence in the mixed bag of seamen he had inherited from Captain Peter Barrow. He dreaded the prospect of having to carry out this operation. It had never entered his head that he might have to try it at night. "It's simple suicide," he thought to himself. Still, orders were orders.

He ordered the helmsman to alter course. Then he called Ruby, and together they went on deck to prepare everything for "part B" so that no time would be lost once they were anchored in the shelter of the rock.

The crew was driven mercilessly. They were not threatened in any way but were simply promised a bonus of two hundred dollars per man for the work they were going to do that night. They did not have to be asked twice. Every single one of them leaped to their tasks as though their very lives were at stake.

The equipment which had been so carefully stowed in the container now was brought on deck. With the help of the ship's derricks and some skillful improvisations, the crew managed to shift the reserve anchor from its place near the forward hatch to the stern of the ship. Under Ruby's directions, other preparations also got underway.

The deposed captain, Peter Barrow, watched the skill

and expertise displayed by Ruby with admiration. The two men had become extremely friendly, despite the fact that the Briton was to all intents and purposes a captive aboard his own vessel. Ruby's three companions, however, were not particularly surprised by the feats of their "master mechanic." They knew him to be a true genius in anything related to machinery or construction. During the period that he had served as vehicle officer of the headquarters reconnaissance unit, legends had grown up about his incredible ability to breathe life into any damaged motor and return it to battle even in the midst of fighting.

There had been that remarkable incident during a commando raid on installations near the Aswan Dam in the heart of Egypt. The Israelis, anxious to get their hands on some highly secret and advanced radar equipment installed there by the Russians, had dropped a raiding party by helicopter. The defending Egyptian forces had resisted fiercely. Right from the start, Ruby's hands had been full. A jeep that had been parked next to a helicopter was badly hit by machine-gun fire. Ruby had it back in working order before the raid was over. Then, in the midst of the shooting, a helicopter on the lit-up field was damaged. A volley of machine-gun bullets ripped into the motor, putting it out of action.

The commander assessed the damage and gave the order to set the machine on fire or blow it up. There was no way of getting it off the ground. He would have to call in another aircraft to help evacuate his troops as well as the equipment they wanted to take back with them. But Ruby was obstinate. He was determined to save the helicopter.

Working single-handed, he made the most remarkable improvisations. When skilled helicopter mechanics examined the machine later, they were at a loss to explain how he had managed to make the plane fly. For that is what he *did* do. With the help of the pilot, who had to perform certain technical maneuvers "to assist me," as Ruby put it, the helicopter not only took off but landed in one piece at its base in Israel.

It was said of Ruby that he could activate any motor of any kind or any make. He knew the secrets of aeronautical and maritime machinery as well as the complicated electronic equipment of modern tanks. He was the "wonder-boy" of the general staff reconnaissance unit of the Mossad.

One of his feats while serving with the Mossad was to break into a highly sophisticated and booby-trapped safe in an east European embassy without the staff suspecting that the raid had even taken place. His initial reluctance to join in the uranium project had nothing to do with a slackening of patriotism or loss of enthusiasm for tackling a difficult and dangerous job. He had joined a kibbutz, and the task he had set himself—that of establishing a plant for the repair and manufacture of agricultural machinery—was just as important as fixing helicopters in the midst of a raid. For Ruby it was just as great a challenge to perform a constructive peaceful job as it was to disconnect an alarm system and outwit a supposedly foolproof combination lock with a bomb attachment. Moreover, he was married and the recent birth of his first son was an important consideration in explaining to the Mossad that he now wanted to spend his days with tractors, not bombs.

In order to enlist his help, Mike had finally had to tell him precisely what the uranium operation entailed. Ruby was forced to agree that there was no one else for the job. He had made up his mind quickly in his two-room apartment on the kibbutz. "I'll come along," he had said simply. "There is no need to discuss it any further." And from that moment on, he had thrown himself heart and soul into the operation.

Now Ruby was hard at work aboard the *Scheersberg A*. It was 8:20 P.M. The rock loomed up in front of them in the darkness.

Chapter Nineteen

The night was clear. Since the NATO plane had buzzed the ship two and a half hours previously, no other aircraft had come in sight.

It was difficult to make out the outline of the "island." Captain Ze'ev Biran used radar and ordered the engine room to reduce speed. Ruby Goldman stayed below to keep an eye on the engineers. As far as he was concerned, they were an unknown quantity. They might be excellent at their work. On the other hand they might be incompetent.

The ship approached the rock slowly. During the previous hour Biran had studied maps and the "Notes to the Mariner" leaflets to determine such details as the direction of the local currents. The massive, jagged mass which now rose before them so sharply from the sea was completely bare. Only an unmanned lighthouse stood on its summit, serving a warning to all shipping in the area to give the rock a wide berth.

Earlier, Ze'ev had asked the bosun to send him the best helmsman aboard. He then transferred the helm from automatic pilot to hand-steering and told the helmsman to take over. The captain now offered up a silent prayer that the man did indeed know his job. The slightest deviation, the merest hesitation in carrying out an order could end in the keel being ripped open by underwater rock, for the charts which Biran had did not provide him with precise and reliable information about the sea bed of the cove or its depth.

As a result, there was only one way for him to operate. The ship would have to edge forward at near zero speed and, with her bows, literally "feel" the depth of the cove. Biran was like a blind man looking for obstacles in a road filled with deep holes, trying to feel his way along with his toes. He was too close now to use radar.

Ze'ev placed two seamen with sticks and ropes by the bulwark of the vessel in the bows and amidships. Their job was to report if the weights hanging at the ends of the ropes touched bottom. He had tried to make use of the depth-finder, but that instrument, like so much of the other equipment on the *Scheersberg*, was unreliable.

He was the first to spot rock formations rising from the waves fifty yards to the left of the bows. Theoretically, they should not have been there. He directed that the searchlight fixed to the left rail of the bridge be focused on the area. The beam bathed the ugly black mass in light.

Gad Ullman was tugging at the captain's sleeve. The navigation lights of another ship were now visible. Ze'ev Biran cursed. He was forced to switch off the searchlights and extinguish every other light he could. They could not afford to be spotted—even if the passing vessel was totally innocent and had nothing to do with the search for the *Scheersberg*.

The anxiety showed in his voice as he told Peter Barrow: "We'll have to get into that hole without lights." The former skipper of the vessel said nothing. He admitted afterward that he considered the maneuver "utterly impossible." At this point, Barrow had a keen professional interest in the operation, and he told Biran he was ready to offer him his "fullest cooperation." Ze'ev thanked him warmly, and for the first time the two men shook hands, right there in the darkness off "rock island" as they called it.

The *Scheersberg* was now too close to the rock to be detected on the radar of another vessel; moreover, visibility was so good that ships in the area might not be using their radar apparatus anyway.

The *Scheersberg* moved slowly, lights doused. They could now hear the constant crash of the waves battering on the island. The sailor with the measuring weights in the bows reported contact with the bottom. "Stop engines," Captain Biran called to Gad Ullman who was standing by the telegraph. Ullman placed the handle of the telegraph in the center of the instrument, opposite the point on the scale marked "Stop." The order to the steersman was given: "Easy to port."

The currents at the entrance to the cove were running too strongly for Captain Ze'ev Biran to stop the ship's movement altogether. He ordered the man at the telegraph to move the handle two degrees forward. "Dead slow ahead," came the command.

If he stopped totally, it was clear that the *Scheersberg* would drift toward the western edge of the rock, colliding disastrously with its outcroppings. By gently keeping the engines working he was able to control the vessel's progress and movement.

Now the sailor sounding out the depth from the left wall of the cargo deck reported touching bottom. Biran promptly ordered the helmsman to turn the bows slightly to the right, but his reaction was a fraction too slow. The *Scheersberg* shuddered and her keel scraped over the rocks.

The voice of Ze'ev was calm and reassuring, despite the anxiety he felt: "Slow astern. Stop. Forward. Easy to starboard . . . to port. Steady as she goes." He *was* the ship. His voice seemed to come from the bowels of the vessel herself, so uncannily did he sense his way forward.

The inlet was so narrow that even a smaller vessel would have required seamanship of the highest quality to enter safely. Almost every possible obstacle that could be found was right there ahead and all around them, ready to wreck the *Scheersberg*. Again and again the ship scraped the bottom. As she did so, every man on board held his breath. The silence was so heavy and oppressive that it seemed to physically press down on all of them.

The entire crew, except for the engine-room squad, were now on deck. Frozen-faced, they watched the rapid maneuverings of the *Scheersberg*. The lifeboats had long been readied for lowering. The more prudent or nervous of the sailors who had no particular duties to perform had stationed themselves close to the lifeboats, trying to do so as inconspicuously as possible.

The ship shook repeatedly. Again and again the keel scraped lightly against the rocky bottom. The man in the bows reported two rocks directly ahead. He was hoarse with fear. The calm stream of instructions from Biran seemed to steady them all. "Easy to port . . . steady as she goes."

The bows rocked a little. The fearful sound of the bottom of the ship grating on rock and sand made every man aboard wince. The engines turned in reverse. Once again the *Scheersberg* freed herself.

Despite the clearness of the night, the inside of the cove, nestling in the shadow of its enormous protective rock, was pitch-dark, as though the island were alive, forbidding man or vessel to penetrate its inky heart. It was impossible to see anything, even from a distance of a few yards. The ship was now being maneuvered virtually blindly, touching rocks and then riding free. Walls of rock enclosed them, sensed rather than clearly seen, and all the more frightening because of their invisibility. The roar of the waves dashing against the rocks echoed and re-echoed all around them. Almost inch by inch the bow of the ship slowly and reluctantly probed forward into the dark and mysterious unknown.

Some special sense warned Ze'ev Biran that the fore half of his vessel was now inside the bay. There was no way of knowing for sure, but that instinct of a true sailor who has the sea in his marrow and who can sense her moods as can a particularly "tuned-in" lover now came to his rescue. As if he had received a vibration of silent warning, Ze'ev suddenly switched on his searchlight. He did not know why he did so, or what particular instinct made him aim at one spot blindly, but that action saved the ship—and possibly all their lives.

The blinding beam of light played full on a sheer rock face fifteen yards in front of them. For the first time, Captain Biran shouted, loud and clear, into the electric bullhorn in his hand: "Let go anchor!"

The bosun, an Austrian named Wolfgang, was standing

dutifully by the windlass. The anchor splashed into the black waters of the bay. The links made a fearful noise, rattling and vibrating as if in violent protest at being let loose in that ominous place. In the engine room the needle of the command telegraph pointed to Dead Slow Astern. Ruby's hand did not leave the fuel valves. The body of the ship again swung forward.

"Stop engines."

The heat in the engine room, compounded by the tension which had seeped below, was searing. The air-conditioning system had never worked after breaking down on the first day. Sweat dripped from Ruby's forehead onto his shirt in a steady stream. He knew if this anchoring operation could be done, Ze'ev was the man to do it, but the question remained—could it be done at all?

The bows made contact with the granite wall. So skillfully had the maneuver been executed that it was more like a gentle kiss than a collision. The ship stopped moving. Biran again shouted into the bullhorn, this time to the stern: "Let go aft anchor!" The rope encircling the anchor ring was freed with a fierce whistling sound, and the anchor was swallowed up by the sea.

A minute later the *Scheersberg A* was stationary. A little bruised and battered perhaps, but at rest. She had aged considerably in the last hour or so, if one were to judge by the "wrinkles" in the form of dents and scratches on her sides and bottom. Now she lay in the center of the inlet. The cove was so small that her stern actually jutted out a little, but the walls of rock to the east and north of her anchorage assured her protection, at least until morning.

Although it was now 10:30 at night, there was no respite for the *Scheersberg*'s crew whose hearts were still pounding from the drama of sailing into the smallest harbor that surely any ship of her size had ever found herself. The entire crew was set to work. The cook, known as "Toni," and the second officer, Christos, at first tried to avoid any physical labor, but they were persuaded to join in with a little not so gentle coaxing from Captain Ze'ev Biran, who showed that beneath the calm exterior he had a very rough nature indeed. He was ably backed by Gad

Ullman who had suddenly decided to give his Beretta a public airing.

Barney MacDowell and Peter Barrow threw themselves into the work with considerably more enthusiasm than might have been expected, considering the circumstances under which they had lost command of the ship. They did not say it aloud, but their professional respect and admiration for the seamanship of Ze'ev Biran was now so unrestrained that they would have done anything to please him. Both men realized that the four "pirates" were Israelis. They had figured out in the broad outline what had happened, and now they were totally caught up in the strange adventure.

Ruby Goldman calculated that they had just ten hours to complete the mission he was in charge of. "Impossible," he said as he looked around him in the bay. Then he got to work.

The first step was to hang the "stages"—painting platforms—over the side on both wings of the ship, as well as in front of the living quarters. The equipment he had brought along for this purpose proved to be very effective. The painting was not done in the usual way with brushes or rollers. It was carried out with the aid of powerful air guns which shot wide jets of paint against the walls of the ship and its superstructure. The men carrying out the operation changed shifts frequently, for the job was exhausting.

This was only part of the renovation program. One of the masts simply vanished. So did two of the Samson posts, the giant ventilation tubes used for bringing air into the holds. Even the gaping holes, which were all that was left of these previously distinguishing features of the *Scheersberg*, had disappeared as though by magic. The gaps were plugged with steel plates painted gray.

By nine in the morning the *Scheersberg* was a new ship. Previously she had been gray. Now her sides were black. With the mast and Samson posts gone, her entire appearance had altered dramatically. The superstructure was also unrecognizable to anyone who had studied the photographs taken the previous evening by the NATO spy plane; instead of being a pale orange, as it had been at the

172

start of the voyage, the superstructure was white now. The dirty orange color of her funnel had changed to blue—a clean, neat blue, a bit streaky in places, it is true, but blue nevertheless. The name of the vessel was also different. She was now the *Kerkyra*.

At dawn the sailors were finally set to work painting the cargo deck green to replace the previous tired gray. (In this case the painting was no luxury, for there had been more rust patches than painted ones.) The faces of the crew were also gray, not from splashed paint but from sheer weariness. They were still hard at it under the watchful eyes of Gad Ullman and Ruby Goldman when a pair of planes were spotted flying low over the northern side of the rock island. Another, quite different plane was seen regularly, once every hour.

A mere thirty minutes after the first aircraft had made an appearance a clearly identified twin-engine reconnaissance aircraft of the French fleet went by. It flew at a considerably higher altitude than the other planes and then disappeared into the blue. "The whole world is looking for us," Pete Barrow said cheerfully to Captain Ze'ev Biran. He made no reply.

At 9:40 in the morning, Ruby announced that the major work was over. In any event they dared not wait any longer. It was daylight now. The 28th of November.

What he saw in the light did not make the Mossad seaman wave his hands in elation. "If I had known last night what I can *see* now," he confided to Peter Barrow, "I would never have even attempted it!" Rocks and outcroppings were evident on all sides of the cove, like the fangs of a beast reaching out hungrily for its prey. The bottom was shallow, the currents strong and swirling, and the waves were high and strong. It was as if they seemed to resent the very presence of the island and were trying to thrust it aside, denying its right to be there at all.

Again Peter Barrow summed up the situation. "Well," he said, "if sailing *in* here was lunacy, then getting out backward is something worse. Suicide I would call it!" He knew that "reversing" in a ship, unless she is fitted with a propeller in the bow, means having to sail without steering. Thus, there is no control over the vessel's course. The *Scheersberg* had no bow's propeller.

Going forward, a ship can be maneuvered left and right, as any amateur seaman knows full well. The current of water along the sides of the ship is caused by the forward movement imparted by the force of the engine. This flow puts pressure on the deflected rudder and prompts the movement of the bow to the left and the right, thanks to the controlled angle of the rudder.

The screws of the *Scheersberg*, like most vessels of her type, have a right-hand turn when sailing forward. Thus they have a left-hand turn when sailing backward. With the ship's steering not functioning, the natural tendency will be for the stern also to deflect to the left, the direction of the spin of the propeller.

The problem seldom arises. Normally, if it were necessary to reverse out of the narrow rocky channel the *Scheersberg* would be aided by a tug. When a tug is not available, then the alternative is to use a powerful steel cable attached to a rigid object. The ship can then be towed backward by working the winches of the derricks. Since no tug was available, the second method had to be tried.

The problem was that nowhere in sight was there a place where a line or steel cable could be attached. There were no hooks or quaysides or suitable pillars of rock which might have served the purpose required to draw the vessel by the stern the eighty yards that separated it from the open sea.

The only option left to Captain Ze'ev Biran, as he knew very well, was to try and make use of the reserve anchor. It would be necessary to cast it into the opening to the cove with two steel cables attached to its head. Then the idea would be to try and stabilize the backward direction of the ship with the help of the two stern winches winding in the steel cables.

The stern winches that the captain was now examining closely were like powerful steel drums. When set parallel, as they were on the *Scheersberg*, and linked to an electric motor by means of a system of cogwheels, they are normally used to tie up the ship in harbor. The process is simple; it is carried out by winding the lines and hawsers of the vessel around the drums with their other ends looped over the bollards on the quayside. The movement is coordinated between the two tying-up points in the bow and stern. The winches work in unison, until the side of the ship is pulled up gently against the quay. As mechanical as the operation is, it requires great engine power.

Captain Ze'ev Biran could only hope that the power of his engines would be sufficient to help pluck the *Scheersberg* out of the bay in which she was trapped. To set the plan in motion he had several crew members build a platform in the form of a wooden raft. They had started shortly before dawn, and now their work was complete. The anchor was raised by means of the tying-up winches and was loaded onto the raft. Ze'ev gave orders for it to be towed by two lifeboats out to the entrance of the cove. The crew was far from enthusiastic. They could hardly be blamed. They had worked tremendously hard all night and they were exhausted now. They balked at getting into the lifeboats.

The reaction enraged Ruby Goldman. Furiously he shouted at them: "All you lazy bastards have to do is lower two small rowboats into the water. Like going on a cruise on a river on a Sunday afternoon. Just tie the anchor to the platform balanced between the two boats. Then go out a few yards into the sea and drop the anchor. I am not asking you to climb to the moon!"

In reality, it was a task that required great skill and alertness under the best of circumstances. And these were not the best of circumstances. Nothing was normal; the sailors were clumsy and lethargic, and work proceeded at an infuriatingly slow pace. The attachment of the anchor to the wooden beamed raft was not easy. The anchor was heavy and awkward. One man nearly crushed his hand while easing it into place, and he had to be replaced by another sailor.

The two lifeboats finally got underway. Their motors were feeble and made slow work of it. As the anchor slid into the sea, the lifeboat to its left capsized and sank like a stone. It was a terrifying experience for all of the men in it, for not a single one of them could swim. Drenched and shivering, they were pulled out of the water and into the second lifeboat and the platform was jettisoned.

Although it was cold, Captain Biran was sweating. Everything was going badly. Again and again he looked anxiously at the sun which seemed to be rising with the speed of a rocket. Within an hour the shadow over the bay would disappear, and any low-flying aircraft could spot them easily. Even though they were now in disguise, the position of a ship in such a strange place would arouse even the most unintelligent of observers.

The lone lifeboat was heading back, slowly and clumsily. Its arrival signaled starkly and clearly just how hazardous the whole anchor enterprise had been. All the men returned safely to the deck of the *Scheersberg*—with one exception. The man left behind in the lifeboat attached the lines from the pelican-shaped hooks with the turning handle to the ring fixed in the fore part of the boat. He then turned to do the same thing in the stern. As he did so, a sudden wave buffeted the boat fiercely, and the sailor's hand was trapped between the two vessels. He lost his balance and fell with the blood-curdling scream into the waters of the bay.

They looked for him in vain. He simply vanished, as though sucked under by a fierce current. Some twenty minutes after the incident his cap was spotted floating near the stern of the *Scheersberg*. They never found his body.

Chapter Twenty

Captain Biran's voice called out sharply: "Heave away."
The cables were tautened with a creaking sound. The
needle of the telegraph moved back. It was dead slow astern. The body of the ship shuddered. The keel was scraping over the top of an underwater reef. Then it was free.
The stern moved slowly out of the hiding place where it
had so reluctantly undergone a face-lift operation during
the hours of darkness. There was no sign of any other
craft on the horizon. The sky, now totally cloudless, was
clear of aircraft.

Captain Ze'ev Biran stood on the left bridge deck. At
his side was Peter Barrow, not interfering but ready with
help or advice if it was required. Gad Ullman was standing in the wheelhouse by the telegraph, gripping its handle
in a steady hand. Under the careful coaching of Biran, he
had been turned into a skilled seaman almost overnight.
The handle of the telegraph was fixed on the red scale at
the point which indicated "Dead Slow Astern." The ship
moved slowly backward. Again the needle was shifted to
the point in the middle of the telegraph—"Stop."

The vessel was moving less by the power of its engines
than by the pulling force of the two winches in the stern.

The bulging drums rotated slowly and the one-inch steel hawsers wound around them with their customary creak of protest. These were the cables normally used for loading cargo with the derricks. Now they had been taken off the pulleys and removed from the derricks. They were carrying out a different task altogether—pulling a ship backward. The two sailors who stood by the winch handles released them at the direct command of the captain.

Two other sailors with depth-seeking weights stood in the stern, on opposite sides to one another. The ropes to which the weights were attached hung from their hands as though they were trying to catch fish using only lines and no rods. They were fairly close to the bridge and their calls could be heard loud and clear. They were tense and shouted out frequently.

Again and again the keel scraped over the underwater rocks. The cables screeched under the strain, as though threatening to snap at any moment. Every shudder of the ship as it touched something sent vibrations along the cable, which alarmed the two men standing by the winch handles—and with good reason.

Peter Barrow looked at Biran. He was like the conductor of a mighty orchestra trying to extract every ounce of musical talent from each player or section in turn. He was a conductor of the utmost virtuosity, thought the deposed skipper. He was young and was learning more about seamanship in this short period than he ever believed possible.

Biran's face showed a tension that was absent from his voice. Sweat was pouring off him as though a bucket of water had been emptied over his head. Yet his commands were calm and controlled, as if he did this sort of thing every day of his life. He paced up and down the bridge from fore to aft with measured tread. His voice was heard clearly from one end of the ship to the other, thanks to the electric bullhorn in his hand. At times he stood absolutely still. Peter Barrow was ready to swear that the man was trying to feel with his feet the whispers or vibrations of whatever it was that the vessel was trying to communicate to him. Barrow was now absolutely convinced that in some mysterious way the *Scheersberg was* talking to Biran, telling him what to do, how to ease her passage out of the hell-hole he had coaxed her into during the hours of darkness.

And all the while the capain kept his eyes on the taut and straining steel cables, as though willing them to carry out his wishes and not snap. Yet again the stern of the ship shook. It was a more violent collision than anything they had experienced up to that time. The cables on the winch drums groaned ominously.

Ze'ev Biran called out to the winch operators: "Stop heaving."

He ordered Gad Ullman to push the telegraph handle forward to "Dead Slow Ahead." The ship failed to respond. She did not move. Again he turned to the winch men and told them to let out the cable. Once more the captain tried to coax the *Scheersberg* forward. But in vain.

He attempted an increase of speed, telling Ullman to put the telegraph handle on "Half Ahead." The body of the ship shuddered and vibrated, but she remained in precisely the same spot. They were stuck. Ze'ev ordered the engines to stop.

Peter Barrow hardly dared breathe. He watched with pounding heart. What was Captain Biran going to do now? For about sixty seconds Biran carefully studied the sea around him, the currents, the winds, the natural direction of the ship. He tried to gaze into the very depths of the sea to work out what his next step would be. They were trapped by a rock reef. Biran asked the two depth-sounders to fathom the reef's depth. Several soundings were made.

"The reef on which we are grounded is not of uniform height," said Ze'ev Biran. Peter Barrow was not quite sure if the captain was simply talking out loud or trying to explain to him what was happening. The Mossad man then went into the wheelhouse to the internal telephone and dialed the engine room. Ruby answered promptly.

Biran did not waste time—or words. "We are stuck on a reef. We'll have to try a little jump. It seems like the only chance. I want you to reverse with everything you've got in one single shot when I give the order. But give it everything there is in those engines of yours. I'll help you all I can with the winches." He paused for a fraction of a second or two, then added: "If we manage to get over this obstacle we are free. Otherwise we are finished."

The captain went back to the left bridge deck and ordered the winch men to wind in the cable slowly. Then, when he heard them tighten and creak against the windlass, he shouted to Gad Ullman: "Full astern. NOW!!!"

The *Scheersberg* vibrated so fiercely it was as though an invisible giant hand was trying to shake it to pieces. Then it seemed to rise up into the air. The shuddering increased. The cables became tauter and quivered. The ship remained rooted to the same spot.

With a roar, Captain Ze'ev Biran screamed to the left winch man, who now looked terrified out of his wits: "For God's sake! More power! Give it more power!"

Instinctively he obeyed. A second later he was flung violently against the side of the ship. With a sound like that of a cannon shot, the cable snapped. It snapped upward in a single movement that was almost too fast for the eye to follow. With a resounding crash it struck the left side of the superstructure, missing the head of the operator by inches. It rebounded, smashing the galley window in the stern of the superstructure.

The winch operator was flung backward, his head striking the iron rail that surrounded his seat. The other winch operator was also hurled forcefully across the deck. The Austrian bosun Wolfgang recovered his wits first. With a single leap he was over the low rail and had landed squarely on the steel deck. In three steps he reached the right winch—the one still in operation.

The two depth-seeking sailors had also been knocked off their feet. Whether they had been struck by the whiplash of the snapped-off cable or had simply collapsed through terror, Captain Ze'ev could not tell from where he was standing. Certainly, by their loud shouts, they were still alive.

But at the moment Ze'ev Biran had lost interest in the two men, for he could feel something else. The ship was sliding backward. Slowly and gently. But moving backward. He had instinctively ducked when the cable snapped. Now, even before he had time to straighten himself up, he shouted out: "Slow astern. Very good. Dead slow. Stop."

The ship was definitely moving backward. She had quite literally "jumped" the reef, like an athlete skimming over a hurdle, scraping it with the underside of his thigh, but leaping over it all the same. Everyone on board now felt the ship move. Her stern swung slowly and consistently to the left. The captain shouted to the right winch man to get to his feet. "For God's sake, get to work!" The sailor was only semi-conscious as he lay sprawled out on the deck. He was obviously not going to take any further part in the maneuver.

The group of rocks now rearing up to the left were getting closer and closer. Far too close for comfort. The right-hand cable was now slack and dangling loose in the water. Biran sensed the double danger facing him. There were the rocks against which they were rapidly drifting, and now there was the cable which might at any minute foul up the screw underwater. Only twenty yards separated the stern from the open sea. But without the pull of the cable it would be impossible to bridge even this gap. There was no control whatsoever over the course of the ship.

The currents in the opening of the bay were powerful and criss-crossed one another. One thing was certain. Unless action was taken quickly, they would dash the *Scheersberg* against the rocks and smash her to pieces. Not only would the uranium go to the bottom, but none of them would survive the experience. The sole lifeboat left to them would not be lowered in time, and even if it was, it would meet the same fate as the ship.

Without the stabilizing pull of the right-hand cable, it was totally impossible to rely on the engine or the ability of the vessel to maneuver. All this passed in a flash through Ze'ev's mind. There was not even time to order someone to take over the winch. Suddenly Captain Biran saw the tall, blond figure of the bosun standing next to the winch handle, and he breathed a mighty sigh of relief.

Wolfgang was a first-class sailor. Ze'ev had spotted that right from the first day that he had taken over the command of the ship. He had been as quick as his captain to see the danger and on his own initiative had taken over the winch. Biran did not have to give the Austrian orders. The cable was wound in rapidly. Now it was doing its job as if it were a tug pulling the *Scheersberg* backward. But it still was not easy. There was only one cable to manipulate—hence half the pull.

To complicate matters the force of the "jump" and the strain of the pulling had ripped the anchor out of its position on the sea floor. The new grip was weak and unstable. The cable had to be manipulated gently, so as not to yank it off the sea bed altogether.

Captain Biran was forced to maneuver the ship back and forth time after time. The *Scheersberg* was tending to drift to the right now, approaching a fresh obstacle of rocks. They were not as large as the ones he had just dodged, but they were almost as dangerous.

The captain now had to order the engines forward to stop from hitting this new rock formation. He hated doing it, since this meant he was heading back for the cove, but he had no choice, for he had to steady the drifting ship. The power of the one remaining winch was not enough to set the *Scheersberg* on a straight course astern.

And so every time the stern approached the rocks to the left, it was necessary for him to move a little forward, to straighten the ship out of her course. It was exhausting, exacting work.

Each time the maneuver was carried out, Captain Ze'ev Biran could see that he had managed to sail the *Scheersberg* astern a mere few feet. He had to repeat the process again and again. One tiny miscalculation could end in disaster. He knew it, and so did Peter Barrow.

Twice more during the course of this tricky operation the ship scraped the surface of the underwater rocks. And now the process of freeing her—"Ahead, astern, steady ..." had to be halted.

An aircraft was heard overhead. "Stop engines," Captain Biran ordered. They all froze where they stood and searched the sky for the plane. It was the same twin-engined military aircraft they had spotted several times during the earlier part of the morning. This time it flew from west to east, at a fairly low altitude, and passed over the rock at a distance of several miles to the south.

The propeller of the *Scheersberg* was silent now. Captain Ze'ev Biran swore to himself that he would shoot any man who tried to signal the plane. He feared that the slightest movement or glint of light would attract the attention of the fliers. He could see the ship's stern once more drifting closer to the rocks, but he did not dare order either the engines or winch into action.

He kept his eye on both the rocks and the plane now disappearing to the east. He could not risk shipwreck any longer. He gave orders for the sea battle to recommence. Once more it was necessary to perform the awkward maneuvers to avoid the rocks.

It was almost noon when they slid out into the sea. It had been two of the most nerve-wracking hours in the naval career of Captain Ze'ev Biran. No matter what he did hereafter in his life, he would never again have his skills so tested to the absolute limit as they had been that morning on the 28th of November, 1968. Instead of feeling tired, he felt a pleasurable glow tingling throughout his body.

"It's made me feel young again," he said aloud to no one in particular. He decided to forgive Mike. Then, quickly remembering that there was still a long way to go before the expedition was over, he ordered the *Scheersberg* —or the *Kerkyra* as she was now called—to turn her bows east-southeast.

Chapter Twenty-one

There was no escaping the aircraft.

At 1:00 P.M. another reconnaissance plane of the French fleet flew low over the area. This time the pilot spotted the small ship. He turned to the left, circled in a slow, wide arc, then dived toward her from astern. Three times he flew over the *Kerkyra*, each run lower than the last "buzzing." Then, almost skimming over the waves, the pilot flew parallel past the left side of the vessel. He was so close that it seemed to the crew that had he come any nearer the plane would strike the vessel with its wing-tips.

From the bridge, Captain Ze'ev Biran could see the heads of the two men in the aircraft. One was staring straight at him through a pair of heavy binoculars. Ruby, who was on the bridge too, waved cheerfully at the pilot. He knew that this was the acid test of his ingenuity. Had he been successful in changing the appearance of the *Scheersberg* sufficiently to fool the world? At least that portion of the world which had set out in pursuit of the ship?

In the broad light of day, Ruby saw for himself some of the slip-ups that had been made and that had been impossible to see at night. The painting of the ship's side had been done virtually blind. That did not matter much. What *did* matter, however, was that the gray steel covers that had been fitted over the gaps left by the removal of the second mast and the air funnels were not a perfect camouflage. They should have been green. He knew that the ship had been carefully photographed; right at this minute experts might be poring over the resultant pictures.

Yet another aircraft came into sight. It passed fairly low. For a moment it seemed that the plane intended to check the profile of the ship from another angle once more. But then it banked sharply to the right, as though the pilot had thought better of it, and a moment later it was a speck in the sky.

At dusk a ship of the United States Sixth Fleet came in sight. It approached and then altered course, as though no longer interested in the *Kerkyra*, and it too vanished over the horizon. The American warship had worried Captain Biran more than the aircraft. Despite the labors of Ruby and the crew, the "cosmetic" work would never stand close scrutiny. The painting was crude. Beneath the layer of black on the ship's side, the traces of the name "Scheersberg A," which had been welded into place, could be seen.

"Not even the four of us can fight off the entire U.S. Sixth Fleet if they decide to board us," Ze'ev Biran muttered to Gad Ullman.

With a perfectly straight face, the "Executioner" said in Hebrew: "We could always use our nuclear deterrent in the hold!"

The captain pretended not to hear. He was still watching the American ship through his binoculars. He dreaded the prospect that it might suddenly change its mind and take another look at the *Kerkyra*, which, if everything had gone according to plan, was by now registered officially in Cyprus.

Finally, turning to Ruby, he said: "I think we have fooled them all—thanks to you. Tonight you can sleep easy."

Ruby Goldman did not argue.

On the 2nd of December an agent of the West German intelligence service reported to its chief, General Gehlen, at headquarters that the *Scheersberg* had docked in the port of Iskenderun in Turkey. The general's instructions were terse but precise: "Try to clarify every possible detail." It took the man only twenty-four hours. His weapon was the simple but highly effective one of gold coins.

Now the agent's answers lay before the German intelligence chief at a meeting called by the security authorities of the Euratom organization. It was such an important gathering that the heads of the secret service sections of several countries, including France, Italy, Switzerland, Holland, and Belgium, were also present, as were other persons whose identities remain unknown to the authors.

The details relayed by the operative did not really make those present any the wiser. There was a very full report about the ship's physical appearance. Her coloring and her structure tallied precisely with another report that had been brought from Antwerp.

Someone, somewhere—quite unknown to the German spy—had decided to undo all Ruby Goldman's work. The *Kerkyra* had vanished from the face of the earth as though by magic. In her place stood the old *Scheersberg*, right down to the "rust" patches and the original mast. (The German operative was not a seaman, and he had no reason to inspect certain items, like the mast, for instance. It was not the original. That was now lying at the bottom of the sea, just off a sheer rock in the waters off Greece.)

When the *Scheersberg* arrived at Iskenderun it was empty. This fact was verified by Lloyds of London, whose agent in Turkey had reported the vessel's docking as a matter of routine. The British secret service had been only too happy to cooperate with its European colleagues. Within minutes of the inquiry, the Germans were told that on its arrival at Iskenderun the *Scheersberg* had declared Naples as its last port of call. From Naples came the following report: "We have no record of any such ship calling here."

According to the German operative, the entire crew of the *Scheersberg A*, captain and all, left their quarters with somewhat indecent haste some two hours after she docked in the Turkish port. His instructions had been to find out all about the ship. Since he was a man who followed orders rigorously, it had never entered his head to try and see what had happened to the *crew*. They had simply vanished.

The Turkish authorities were also cooperative, but they could come up with no answers. Why should anyone have bothered to try and see what the crew of just another ship were up to when they stepped ashore? The local brothels were asked if they could remember anything unusual, but to them one sailor was like another. How should they know from which ships the clients of the preceding days had come?

On the 5th of December an entirely new crew arrived to take over the *Scheersberg*. Until then the vessel had lain like a ghost in the harbor. This had not caused any concern in the port area since the harbor fees had been paid in advance.

The new crew, who were predominantly Spanish, explained to the curious gentleman who spoke their language with a German accent that they had been laid off in Rotterdam on the 15th of November. To their surprise, they were kept on payroll and were instructed to remain in Holland; the owner had been so "happy with their services that he was trying to find the lot of them a new job." Their contact was a Herr Fritz Kopke of Kajen Quay, Hamburg. Investigators could find no trace of him.

The crew explained that the only men missing from the original crew were the captain and the first officer, who were "English or Scottish, or something like that," and the second officer, whom they remembered was named Christos. According to their latest instructions, they were to take on board a cargo of beans and salt, and proceed to Palermo.

The German agent had been thorough. He had boarded the ship and taken a look at the logbook, which he planned to photograph. It was a futile exercise. Most of the pages for the previous two and a half weeks had been ripped out. The engine room log also provided no clues. Although only some of these pages were ripped out, the others were so covered with oil stains that it was impossible to decipher a single word.

In the days that followed, a close watch was kept on the vessel, but General Gehlen knew this was a waste of time. The holds of the *Scheersberg* were empty. There was no

trace of uranium there—or of anything else for that matter. His operative in Iskenderun was absolutely certain
about that.

From Turkey the vessel made its way to Palermo. It
then sailed westward and finally arrived in Denmark just
after Christmas. But these details were totally unimportant. The question remained: What had happened to the
Scheersberg between the time she left Antwerp on the 17th
of November and the time she arrived in Iskenderun on
the 2nd of December? How had she spent those missing
fifteen days?

Part of the answer lay on the desks of the intelligence
chiefs. She *had* been spotted by aircraft heading eastward
in the Mediterranean on the evening of the 27th of
November. Another plane had taken a routine picture of
her more to the west two days previously, but this was by
chance, for at that time no one was looking for the
Scheersberg. The photographs were beautiful pieces of
aerial "spy work." Even the name was legible. And in case
there was doubt in anyone's mind, the photos had been en-
larged; the name "*Scheersberg A*" stood out boldly and
clearly.

From that time on, despite the efforts of the entire
NATO force in the Mediterranean, the vessel had simply
vanished, "as though swallowed up by one of those myth-
ical Greek sea-dragons," said one of the investigators
dryly.

None of the intelligence men had any illusions about
what had happened. When last seen, the *Scheersberg* was
heading straight east. They did not even have to refer to
their maps; to the east lay the Israeli port of Haifa. And
to the north of Haifa, just a comfortable day's sailing for
the vessel, was the Turkish port of Iskenderun. It did not
require the help of experts for all of them to work it out.

The Dutch secret service man present, who did not care
much for his French counterpart, looked at him and asked
with a straight face: "I wonder why they would want
uranium? Don't they get supplies from you?"

The Frenchman let it pass. He was not going to rise to
the bait. In any event, he disagreed totally with President
de Gaulle's policies in general, and in particular with the
way he had stabbed the Israelis in the back with his em-

bargo ruling. Like most members of the French military and security services he disliked Arabs, in part a legacy of the bitter war fought in Algeria against the FLN rebels.

Enrico Jacchia, an important official at Euratom, was in the hot seat at the meeting, and he was having a hard time suppressing his anger.* Although his title was "Director of Preventive Medicine," he was actually the man in charge of security arrangements.

Again and again he had warned about the inadequate security arrangements at Euratom. Bureaucratic delays and petty jealousies among officials, who were more concerned with national prestige than with total efficiency, had blocked suggestions for tighter controls.

Euratom members all knew Jacchai to be an honest and intelligent official who was trying to do a very important job, and they sympathized with him. He had to operate openly and officially, and that meant that he was working with one hand tied behind his back and the other not permitted free action.

"What is the significance of all this?" one man asked bluntly.

An expert responded: "Israel has at this time a relatively small twenty-six megawatt reactor acquired from France. We are not absolutely sure of the work they are doing at their reactor station at Dimona. It is my view that when

---

*In June, 1977, when the affair came to light, Enrico Jacchia leaped to the defense of his role in the disappearance of the "plumbat," as he called it.

"We wasted months in making requests and getting elusive responses. We were forced to comply with Euratom's procedural rules. A year after the incident, in November, 1969, I was finally able to outline the developments of the 'plumbat affair.' The ways to cheat international safeguards are innumerable, like the ways of the Lord. They can be devised in a manner that is most appropriate to the particular situation.

"The 'plumbat affair' was conducted in a perfectly legal manner until the crucial moment—the exit of the *Scheersberg* from the port of Antwerp into international waters. This was when the captain could freely sail his ship, not to the port of Genoa, which had been authorized by the competent authorities of all the countries concerned, but to its real and planned destination. It was not an act of aggression in the open seas. It was a nonviolent, intelligent interpretation of the Euratom treaty's procedural rules."

Jacchia complained that only after the incident was the "safeguards staff" increased from "15 to 100 persons."

189

the French government cut off the necessary supplies of uranium, Israel had an urgent need for a fresh source of fuel. The reactor at Dimona in the Negev Desert is a heavy-water device which works off natural unenriched uranium. To the best of my knowledge—and my French friend here might be able to tell me differently, although I doubt it, the type of uranium that vanished from the *Scheersberg A* is just the type of fuel they needed.

"The reactor produces about twenty kilograms of weapon-grade plutonium a year. Provided the scientific and technological know-how is available, this is sufficient to make two or three nuclear devices a year, each equivalent to 20,000 tons of TNT. This is about the size of the bomb dropped on Nagasaki. The Israelis do have skilled scientists. My calculations are, therefore, that the two tons of uranium which have vanished are capable of eventually making between twenty or thirty bombs."

There was total silence in the room. Then the pressure was put on General Gehlen. The Frenchman seated beside the head of the French security service had not been exactly welcome, but it was decided by the occupant of the Elysée Palace that he attend the meeting. His anti-Israel stance was well known. His secret service chief sat in stony silence; the look of suppressed fury on his face was far more eloquent than any words.

"Now is the time to prevent it," said the politician sharply. He looked at the aging German general. "You have a special relationship with the United States. With the aid of this connection you can insist that the Israelis return the uranium to its rightful owners—whoever they are," he added with biting sarcasm as he glanced at the Euratom representative.

The German had never made any secret of his pro-American sentiments, nor of his close links with the CIA. If he was tempted to score a point against this officious French administrator, he resisted it. How easy it would have been to say: "Since your 'independent' stand against NATO, and your coolness toward the United States, I am surprised that you want to ask them for any favors!"

This was not the tack he took, however. His voice was weak, for he was an old man, but even so, his thoughts were lucid and clear. Every man in the room sat listening intently.

"It would be a fatal error to turn to the Americans right now. You know as well as I that since Euratom was formed, they have regarded this organization with the utmost suspicion for a variety of reasons. It challenges their exclusive nuclear status in the West. They see it as a rival, both commercially and in other ways. They would be very happy to drive a stake into its heart."

He paused and looked at the French official: "If we approach them now and make a request for their help, we will be at their mercy. It will be admitting that we have failed to do our job of looking after our own nuclear resources and fuel, or whatever."

His voice deepened now, and he asked cuttingly: "Is *that* what you want?"

The Frenchman argued hotly. The General was soft-voiced as he responded: "If it were only a question of the stolen shipment, then I would not be concerned. Indeed, you are right, it might be the best method of getting the uranium returned. Although I am not so sure. You know that the Israelis have a powerful voice in the United States. There are a lot of Jews in New York. It would be awkward for Washington to start twisting little Israel's arm. I needn't point out to you that there is a great wave of admiration still sweeping the world as a result of the Israeli victory in the Six-Day War." The German could not resist it now: "In spite of everything."

The barb went home, as everyone who glanced at the Frenchman could see. The "In spite of everything" was the French embargo, which might have, but did not, cripple the Israeli war effort. They had won despite the bullying by President de Gaulle.

Now the German's voice rose again: "I am not going to do it." He was firm and decisive. "For I am above everything else a German patriot, and a dedicated European. To speak to the United States would be to betray the interests of my country and the whole of Europe."

The decision of the gathering was unanimous. Unanimous, for the French voice of the Elysée Palace at the meeting left before it was over. He knew that he would only be humiliated if he remained any longer.

The affair was to be hushed up.* Officially the United States was not to be told.

Two months after the death of the "old fox," as they admiringly called the head of the German intelligence service, the CIA was given an unexpected present. It was a secret file from the private archives of the general, and it was transferred to the CIA as the last wish of the dying Gehlen.

In it, American agents read the full story of the disappearance of the *Scheersberg A*. There were details of the hijacking, the identity of the men involved, the stages that preceded the disappearance of the 560 barrels of yellowish ore. The file disclosed that at the meeting to find out what happened to the "yellowcake" and what to do about it, the general had not revealed everything he really knew to his colleagues. There was no indication that the German secret service was directly involved. The CIA drew its own conclusions, however.

In January, 1977, President Carter was sworn in as the thirty-ninth President of the United States. One of his first steps was to try and increase American control of the world trade in fissionable material, and thus limit its uncontrolled spread throughout the world.

Enrico Jacchia leaped immediately to the defense of the American President. In his new role as general director of the European Community, this former chief of nuclear safeguards said: "The American President is right. Jimmy Carter is right on moral as well as political grounds."

Did the President have the "plumbat incident" in mind? Was it mere coincidence that in April, 1977, Mr. Paul Leventhal, a former U.S. Senate expert on nuclear proliferation, told the world about the disappearance of the uranium aboard the *Scheersberg A*—an incident that had occurred eight and a half years earlier? It was the first time the public had ever heard of the matter. It looked as though the well-known tactic of John Foster Dulles was being employed by the new President: the technique of controlled leakage of news.

*Following the inquiry held by Euratom, certain officials of the organization resigned. The findings of this inquiry are top secret.

OPERATION URANIUM SHIP

To coincide with the "revelation" by Paul Leventhal, three of the largest U.S. dailies, *The New York Times,* the *Washington Post,* and the *Los Angeles Times,* published the scoop that reverberated all around the world:

ISRAEL PERFORMS NUCLEAR ENTEBBE

A cargo of 200 tons of uranium on its way from West Germany to Italy disappeared mysteriously in a brilliant diversion operation and reached the Israeli atomic reactor at Dimona. This cargo is sufficient to produce thirty nuclear bombs.

The Israeli Atomic Energy Commission immediately denied any Israeli connection with the disappearance of the uranium. Israel has said all along that the uranium it needs for the Dimona reactor is obtained as a by-product from the phosphate plants standing next to the Dead Sea.

Not far from the nuclear reactor at Dimona stands the extraordinary rock of Masada, where Jewish zealots defied the attempts of the mighty Roman army to conquer them. From their fortress on top of this squat, flat-topped rock which dominates the Dead Sea a few hundred men, women, and children held out for three years. And when they were about to be overcome, rather than surrender their status as free people, they killed themselves in an awe-inspiring mass suicide.

Today Israeli tank crew and other armored unit officers hold their swearing-in parade ceremonies on the rocky summit of Masada. It is a deliberate demonstration that, far from the quiet, passive spirit of the Jews who marched to their deaths in concentration camp gas chambers, the Israelis of today are filled with the same spirit of heroism and courage that marked the patriots of Masada.

Epilogue

It has not been possible to give all the names of the men and women involved in the uranium affair. We have been asked not to reveal certain secrets, and there are other secrets that are not known to the authors.

General Meir Amit left the security services a short time after the *Scheersberg* "disappeared" for fifteen days. It was one of the greatest intelligence coups that had been carried out since he took over from Isser Harel, the man who built the Mossad into one of the most highly regarded intelligence services in the world. Amit went into politics eventually, and today he is a member of the Knesset—the Israeli Parliament.

Professor Benjamin Bentheim is not his real name. He is still a key figure at Dimona.

Mike still works for the Mossad. His real name is not even known to his closest friends. He has never been photographed.

Reuven (Ruby) Goldman is the manager of a highly successful agricultural implements plant at a kibbutz. Since the *Scheersberg* affair he has twice been called in by Mike to take part in secret operations where his expertise was needed.

Benny Arnheim is still the number one communications expert at Mossad headquarters.

Captain Ze'ev Biran commands a ship of the Israeli merchant fleet. Mike kept his word to him. Since the uranium escapade, he has not been called on to carry out similar missions. His love for the sea is, if anything, greater today than it has ever been.

Gad Ullman was killed on a secret service mission on October 18, 1973.

Sharon Masters is married. She has retired from the Mossad.

Antonio Bordini is not his real name; he did work for Euratom. Two months after the *Scheersberg* sailed from Antwerp, he simply disappeared from his place of business. His present whereabouts are unknown. He and Sharon did not marry.

Bikbashi Fuad Abdul Nasser, at his own request, returned to Egypt a few hours after the news was brought to him that Colonel Habib Boudija had been found with a broken neck in Brussels. His name has not been heard of since in international intelligence circles.

General Muhammed Ofkir did not have to answer to the king about the uranium ship disaster, for the monarch knew nothing about it in the first place. Later, however, the general plotted his own coup against the king in an attempt to take over the country. Two pilots in French Super Mystères were sent up over Rabat airport to shoot down the royal aircraft, but the skill of the king's pilot, the poor shooting of the plotters, and some incredibly good luck enabled King Hassan II to escape. He did not torture or even imprison the general, for he had genuinely loved him as a brother. Instead he offered Ofkir the honorable way out. Ofkir, ever the French-trained officer, shot himself.

The bodies of *Meir Azoulai* and *Shauli Mizrachi* were brought home to Israel for burial at a military cemetery in Haifa after they were exchanged for the bodies of the six dead Egyptians who met their end in Antwerp.

Captain Peter Barrow was offered a job on an Israeli ship. He accepted, but during the past eight and a half years he has skippered other vessels as well. This is not his real name, for obvious reasons. Some of the other sailors were also given jobs on Israeli ships.

Herbert Scharf, the man who created the Asmara company, told the authors: "I know nothing about uranium deals." The Asmara company was dissolved in 1975.

Herbert Schulzen, the purchasing agent for Asmara, is today working for Kolloid Chemie, a West German company concerned with the manufacture and sale of dye materials for industry. Although he admits that the "secret services" were involved in the shadowy Asmara company, he told *Time* magazine (May 30, 1977): "When I read in the papers that for nine years various governments have kept the disappearance of the uranium a secret, I cannot as a private individual comment on what is taking place at a higher political level."

Biscayne Traders Shipping Corporation, which was set up as a Mossad "front," was registered in Monrovia, Liberia, on August 20, 1968; on September 27, 1968, it took legal possession of the uranium ship. One of the men who was listed as a director and president of the corporation was *Dan Ert*. Although Ert was not actually involved in the uranium ship episode, he was a member of a Mossad squad which, in 1973, assassinated an Arab waiter in the Norwegian city of Lillehammer in the belief that the man was a terrorist. Ert served less than two years in a Norwegian jail for his part in this operation. He now lives in Israel where he is known by his Hebrew name, Dan Aerbel. He has never discussed any aspect of his secret service career.

The *Scheersberg A* is today the *Kerkyra*. Lloyds of London, which registers the names of ships and their journeys, has a long record of her voyages after reaching the Turkish port of Iskenderun on December 2, 1968. The ship was sold by Biscayne in 1970 to a Greek shipping line which in turn sold the vessel to another shipping line six years later. Today she tramps the Mediterranean under the name *Kerkyra*. A remnant of her glamorous past still remains: the outline of her original name, which is faintly discernible beneath the paint on her side.

Big Bestsellers from SIGNET

☐ **RUNNING AWAY by Charlotte Vale Allen.**
(#E7740—$1.75)

☐ **THE ACCURSED by Paul Boorstin.** (#E7745—$1.75)

☐ **THE RICH ARE WITH YOU ALWAYS by Malcolm Macdonald.** (#E7682—$2.25)

☐ **THE WORLD FROM ROUGH STONES by Malcolm Macdonald.** (#J6891—$1.95)

☐ **THE FRENCH BRIDE by Evelyn Anthony.**
(#J7683—$1.95)

☐ **TELL ME EVERYTHING by Marie Brenner.**
(#J7685—$1.95)

☐ **ALYX by Lolah Burford.** (#J7640—$1.95)

☐ **MACLYON by Lolah Burford.** (#J7773—$1.95)

☐ **FIRST, YOU CRY by Betty Rollin.** (#J7641—$1.95)

☐ **THE DEVIL IN CRYSTAL by Erica Lindley.**
(#E7643—$1.75)

☐ **THE BRACKENROYD INHERITANCE by Erica Lindley.**
(#W6795—$1.50)

☐ **LYNDON JOHNSON AND THE AMERICAN DREAM by Doris Kearns.** (#E7609—$2.50)

☐ **THIS IS THE HOUSE by Deborah Hill.** (#J7610—$1.95)

☐ **THE DEMON by Hubert Selby, Jr.** (#J7611—$1.95)

☐ **LORD RIVINGTON'S LADY by Eileen Jackson.**
(#W7612—$1.50)

THE NEW AMERICAN LIBRARY, INC.,
P.O. Box 999, Bergenfield, New Jersey 07621

Please send me the SIGNET BOOKS I have checked above. I am enclosing $_____(check or money order—no currency or C.O.D.'s). Please include the list price plus 35¢ a copy to cover handling and mailing costs. (Prices and numbers are subject to change without notice.)

Name_____

Address_____

City_____State_____Zip Code_____
Allow at least 4 weeks for delivery

Have You Read These Bestsellers from SIGNET?

- [ ] **ROGUE'S MISTRESS by Constance Gluyas.**
  (#J7533—$1.95)
- [ ] **SAVAGE EDEN by Constance Gluyas.** (#J7681—$1.95)
- [ ] **LOVE SONG by Adam Kennedy.** (#E7535—$1.75)
- [ ] **THE DREAM'S ON ME by Dotson Rader.**
  (#E7536—$1.75)
- [ ] **SINATRA by Earl Wilson.** (#E7487—$2.25)
- [ ] **THE WATSONS by Jane Austen and John Coates.**
  (#J7522—$1.95)
- [ ] **SANDITON by Jane Austen and Another Lady.**
  (#J6945—$1.95)
- [ ] **THE FIRES OF GLENLOCHY by Constance Heaven.**
  (#E7452—$1.75)
- [ ] **A PLACE OF STONES by Constance Heaven.**
  (#W7046—$1.50)
- [ ] **THE ROCKEFELLERS by Peter Collier and David Horo-witz.** (#E7451—$2.75)
- [ ] **THE HAZARDS OF BEING MALE by Herb Goldberg.**
  (#E7359—$1.75)
- [ ] **COME LIVE MY LIFE by Robert H. Rimmer.**
  (#J7421—$1.95)
- [ ] **THE FRENCHMAN by Velda Johnston.**
  (#W7519—$1.50)
- [ ] **THE HOUSE ON THE LEFT BANK by Velda Johnston.**
  (#W7279—$1.50)
- [ ] **A ROOM WITH DARK MIRRORS by Velda Johnston.**
  (#W7143—$1.50)

THE NEW AMERICAN LIBRARY, INC.,
P.O. Box 999, Bergenfield, New Jersey 07621

Please send me the SIGNET BOOKS I have checked above. I am enclosing $_____(check or money order—no currency or C.O.D.'s). Please include the list price plus 35¢ a copy to cover handling and mailing costs. (Prices and numbers are subject to change without notice.)

Name_____

Address_____

City_____ State_____ Zip Code_____
Allow at least 4 weeks for delivery

More Big Bestsellers from SIGNET

☐ **THE MANLY-HEARTED WOMAN** by Frederick Manfred.
(#E7648—$1.75)

☐ **WHITE FIRES BURNING** by Catherine Dillon.
(#E7351—$1.75)

☐ **CONSTANTINE CAY** by Catherine Dillon.
(#E7583—$1.75)

☐ **FOREVER AMBER** by Kathleen Winsor.
(#E7675—$2.25)

☐ **SMOULDERING FIRES** by Anya Seton.
(#J7276—$1.95)

☐ **HARVEST OF DESIRE** by Rochelle Larkin.
(#J7277—$1.95)

☐ **THE GREEK TREASURE** by Irving Stone.
(#E7211—$2.25)

☐ **THE GATES OF HELL** by Harrison Salisbury.
(#E7213—$2.25)

☐ **KINFLICKS** by Lisa Alther.   (#E7390—$2.25)

☐ **ROSE: MY LIFE IN SERVICE** by Rosina Harrison.
(#J7174—$1.95)

☐ **THE FINAL FIRE** by Dennis Smith.   (#J7141—$1.95)

☐ **SOME KIND OF HERO** by James Kirkwood.
(#J7142—$1.95)

☐ **CBS: Reflections in a Bloodshot Eye** by Robert Metz.
(#E7115—$2.25)

☐ **THE GOLDEN SONGBIRD** by Sheila Walsh.
(#W6639—$1.50)

☐ **MADALENA** by Sheila Walsh.   (#W7457—$1.50)